I MARRIED AN EX-WISE GUY

Our Life, Love and His Death Together

SELIA SUNSHINE

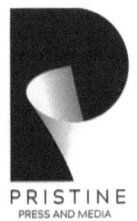

PRISTINE
PRESS AND MEDIA

ISBN
978-1-964804-01-9 (Paperback)
978-1-964804-00-2 (eBook)
978-1-964804-02-6 (Hardcover)

I MARRIED AN EX-WISE GUY

Our Life, Love and His Death Together

SELIA SUNSHINE

TABLE OF CONTENTS

CHAPTER 1

—×—

Big Guy Made Her Smile

She got home and went directly to the tiny second bedroom of her apartment that was shared with a small, glass-top desk and her laptop. Even though she was weary from drinking too many margaritas the night before and driving home from Rocklin for two and a half hours, she had to get her thoughts down on paper. The playoff game between the Ravens and Steelers was just getting started, but she passed it up in favor of her thoughts. They were important to her and more important than the football game. This was an unusual thing for her to do.

The long drive was one of the few pleasant times she has had in well over a year or two or three. She smiled all along the way. Smiled so long and so hard her face was hurting. Often, she had to shake her head to wake her mind up to the reality of what was going on. She was driving west at 75 miles per hour down Hwy. 80 on her way back to Tomales - not still in Reno with a tall, handsome, gentle, hunk of a man. She kept telling herself to pay attention to the road or she would miss the Lakeville Hwy. turnoff.

Nevertheless, she could not get her mind off the romantic encounter she just had and all the things that happened to get her to such an encounter that made her smile. This was number one on the list of pleasant memories in the last year or two or three. All the thoughts swirled and swirled through her memory bank, starting from the day she met a man named Tim.

Hello Mr. Tipton, it's Selia. I'm a little bit early and will be outside at the Valet waiting for you. I will be the one with the gray hair and a silver sun visor.

After hanging up she thought about how much she hated cell phones but knew they were a necessary evil when trying to make a living in the real estate business. She looked around and wondered what the hell she was doing at the valet parking area at Harrah's, Laughlin, when she should really be at home.

First of all, she didn't really have to make a living. Between her husband's social security, her PERS retirement and a few other investments they had made, there was enough to cover all expenses and some left over for fun. Besides, her husband was very ill and would probably not be around much more than a couple of years. She wished she were with him right now. He insisted she keep active - so there she stood waiting for a man she had only met on the telephone.

And what a meeting it was. When he did not get a return phone call immediately, he chewed her out royally when they finally talked. Once he found out why his call was returned later than usual, he became a nice, soft-spoken person.

Her apprehension grew while waiting - which person was she going to meet in person.

She finally noticed two men walking toward her - one man was very tall and robust, the other was average looking and in stature. Oh My - was her first thought. The big man extended his hand and introduced himself as Tim and then introduced his buddy, Robert.

Her mind flashed back to her last boyfriend, Sean, and her crotch started to throb. Sean was a big man too and Tim had the same confident, swagger that she recalled about Sean. She wondered if the throb stemmed from thinking of Sean. How making love with him was great; whether because of her husband having had his prostate removed three years earlier due to cancer and the "deed" was no longer part of their marital bed, which she missed, or did this big man named Tim stir a physical reaction in her because she was just flat out horny due to "all of the above."

She turned away from the two men standing there, blinked her eyes over and over in order to take her mental focus away from sex, and then showed them to her truck. She spent the day driving the two men around Valley of Flowers, Arizona, looking at properties. All in all, it was a pleasant day and a great diversion from her usual tasks of changing oxygen tanks and dispensing medications to her husband.

The big guy was the chatty one. His chatter was light, but meaningful. He was great at getting her to talk about herself, without her even realizing it. He sat in the front seat next to her in the driver's seat and his strong manly voice continued to stir up her libido. The "average guy" did not say much at all. She wondered if they were a "couple." By the end of the day, Mr. Average finally started conversing. That's when she found out that Mr. Average had a lady friend in Seattle where both guys lived. She was really relieved to find that out because it felt creepy thinking a "big gay guy" could turn her on.

Upon arriving back at Harrah's, she got out of the truck to say goodbye and all the keep in touches, will let you knows, and all the usual platitudes of a professional realtor. Instead of extending his hand, the big guy thanks her for her time by giving her a huge bear hug. She did not expect this and, damn, there goes that throbbing again.

CHAPTER 2

—×—

Her Memories Overtake

The months go by slowly and the times are changing for her. Three more trips to the emergency room with her husband because of pneumonia and the real estate market falls in the crapper. The only contact with the big guy was throug!h email and only to send him listings of property. She never thought of the flashing moments of heightened libido when she first met the big guy named Tim as she was too busy taking care of her husband. Nothing of that sort seemed important to her now. Her days were taken up with dispensing medications, along with morphine and emptying catheter bags.

The impending passing of her husband was very apparent now. She thought back to his last birthday and how she regrets not doing for him what he really wanted that day. After getting him comfortable in his hospital bed, she sat down to watch television in the room and her mind drifted back to their crazy, romantic beginning.

It was happy hour on Friday night at Sam's Club in Marin County. She started going there because she previously dated the owner, but after nine months of dating him, she broke it off. She did not like being told how to think and what to say and no matter how much money the man had, she was not about to let him change her in any way. She felt like all she was to him was "arm candy." Even though she was no longer seeing Sam, she continued going there on Friday nights because she had fun with all the new people she had met there.

It was a typical happy hour with the hors d veers on a buffet table in the café part of the bar. All the usual three-piece- suiters and hard hats were already in attendance when she arrived about 5:30 in the evening. She liked sitting around the corner of the bar on the last barstool. This gave her an advantage to scope out the entire bar and all the patrons as they came in or left. She was hoping to see the handsome stranger that she had seen come in a few times before but never had the guts to approach him.

He seemed very different from the others that frequented Sam's. He was always dressed in slacks, dress shirt and tie and, depending on the weather, had on either a jacket length London Fog trench coat, or a full-length one. He had an aura that was very smooth but mysterious and she wanted to know more about this man. His posture was straight up and he walked with slow, purposeful steps. It almost seemed as if "the red sea was being parted" when he came through the door. This mysterious man had a commanding presence and everyone always noticed him when he walked in. She was determined to find out who he was and what his story was as soon as she got the courage up.

She began to chatter with someone sitting next to her when the bartender needed to get out from behind the bar. Instead of lifting the section of the bar that had the hinge opening, he just went under. She took the opportunity to be silly and said to the bartender "while you're down there, do an old lady a favor." Little did she know the handsome stranger had come into the Club when she was not paying attention to the comings and goings at the entrance she had been keeping an eye on. People were three deep at the bar by then and he was standing directly behind her. She looked at him and sheepishly grinned while turning a little red. She asked him if he heard what she said and he beamed with a big smile and said "Oh Yes."

Because it was late fall, actually it was November 1992, the darkness set in early and people were ready to get their weekend started with some heavy partying. He bought her a drink as they exchanged small talk. She found herself looking deep into his big, round blue eyes and listening to his smooth voice. His silver, wavy hair shined under the small light above them. She became aware immediately that he was a smooth talking lady's man who knew all the right things to say. It did not matter to her – she was eating it up and loving every minute of it. Little did she realize it was not minutes, it was hours that were going by. By then she learned his name was James, was single, his place of employment was down the road a short distance and he moved from New York, to Contra Costa County because his mother was very ill and his sister talked him into coming back to California.

The jukebox was playing and couples were dancing. The handsome stranger extended his hand and asked her to dance. Boy, oh boy, oh boy, did it feel good being in the arms of this handsome stranger named James. There was a genuine gentle, masculine quality about the way this mysterious man held her and she just melted into his body as they danced slow dance after slow dance. With each passing dance, their bodies became closer and closer and they began to move as one.

It was getting close to midnight. In her "single Dom" whenever she went out to a pub, especially where a live band was playing, she always got there by eight o'clock, got the perfect spot at the bar that gave her full view of everything and then left at midnight. This way she had a good time dancing, had a few drinks and was not in danger of taking home a 10 and waking up with a 2. When the music stopped, she told James she was going to leave and how nice it was to meet him. He reciprocated with the pleasantries and asked her if she would drop him off at his car, which was just down the road at his office. He obviously had a plan.

CHAPTER 3

—×—

The Electricity Continues

He followed her to her car. It was a 2-seater, Penninfarina (aka Fiat Spider 2000). She felt pretty safe because there is not much you can do in a small sports car. Upon a!rriving at the parking lot where his car sat in the total darkness of an industrial parking lot, he reached over and cupped the sides of her face with his strong masculine hands. She knew what was coming and did not fear it at all. She turned the ignition off on the car and welcomed his mouth to hers.

Many, long, caressing kisses brought the two to an excitement they dared not reach while dancing in the public area at the bar. With the darkness of the parking lot and finally being alone, neither one of them could stop. The slow probing of their tongues worked together in perfect unison. She could not remember ever being so overtaken by a kiss from a man. She did not want it to end.

He gently placed her left hand between his legs and caressed it with his thighs. The massaging he was receiving was no longer enough. He released his hardness from the zipper of his slacks and the pocket of his briefs and softly guided her mouth to him. Her arousal level was up to the star lit sky, at that point, so she approached his bodily request with enthusiasm.

Very little oral stimulation was required before his body stiffened and shook. Soft whispers of "Oh my god, oohhh my god, ooohhhh" were blurted out over and over again as his body slowly softened and eased back into the seat.

He cupped her face again and brought her to him. His strong arms enveloped her completely and she just lay against his chest as he stroked her hair and face for what seemed like a very long time.

The tightness of the small car made the gearshift dig into her side, so, as much as she did not want the caressing to end, she told him she really needed to just go home. He asked for her phone number, said good night and got into his own vehicle.

She drove home saying aloud to herself, "Oh my god, Oh my god, where has this man been all my life."

CHAPTER 4

—×—

The Romance Begins

A stirring noise and moaning in the hospital bed brings her back to reality. She kisses her husband on the cheek. After all the time she just spent down memory lane, she feels a stirring and regrets even more she did not take care of his birthday wish.

She sees to his needs and brings him his finger food that she prepares twice weekly. Finger food, at that point in his life, was what was easiest for him to eat without having to be fed by someone else. She worked hard so that he could maintain his dignity. When he finished, she petted him, gave him some morphine, made sure he drank lots of water, and then settled him down into bed. The effort to sit up, eat and drink was exhausting for him.

The effort it took her to watch her once virile husband die was excruciating for her. She settled back again and mentally wandered back into memory lane beginning where she had left off after their first meeting.

She remembered giving him her work phone number and was surprised to hear from him on Monday morning.

She answered her telephone her usual way. It was her private line so only people that already knew her used that line. "Hi, this is Selia." She immediately recognized the voice and blushed. She commented that she was glad he had called as she figured he wanted to apologize for the events of Friday night. He was very adamant that was not the reason he was calling. He said he called to let her know that it was wonderful to meet her and hoped to see her again.

Now she felt foolish and agreed to meet him at Sam's Club again. Things progressed to a full-blown romance quickly. They met there often, had dinner together and stayed at several local hotels often. She liked the fact that he did not sleep with his socks on. That would have been a real turn off. She found him to be extremely comfortable to sleep alongside. She was 5' 8" tall and he was 5'11". Their bodies meshed perfectly because she was very long legged and his were short. This meant their bodies could curl up together perfectly. He was a hugger, which she liked very much and he liked going to sleep with his arm over her shoulder. This was the first time in her life that her lover's arm never seemed to get heavy through the night. His lovemaking was the most gentle, caring and giving she had ever experienced.

They were getting to know each other. He boasted about being proud that the most important aspect of love making for him was to make his partner happy. And that he did. His "oral" skills were right on point and never failed him. His use of his hands was incredible and his male hardness was quite adequate.

As the weeks went by, she became increasingly enthralled with the handsome stranger named James. At age 46, she was no longer the naïve, lovelorn (lust actually) idiot who married her second husband after only knowing him for two weeks. This attraction had little to do with what he had to say. Often what he said appeared to be so bizarre she just shook her head and thought he was a little bit goofy. But, it didn't matter. It was his swagger, his way of hugging, kissing and being an old fashion gentleman in every way. She ate up every minute they spent together because his attention was only on her at all times. This is a fact that she did not realize until after his death when she told her daughter about his passing she starting sobbing and gasped out that he loved you so much, all he ever thought about was you mom.

It was close to Christmas time by now. They continued to meet at Sam's Club and stay at a local hotel. She did not have him over to her house yet because her 22 year old son had moved back in until he could find a job.

The after work customers at Sam's Club started to accept the fact that this man who they had only stared at in the past when he walked in the door, was now a regular hanging out with Sam's ex-girlfriend. Most of the men still kept their distance from him, especially, Jim, her golf instructor. Their eyes would meet, but they never said a word to each other. This was the beginning of her realization that maybe he was not as goofy as she thought or at the least, there was definitely something different about this man. Later in their relationship, she would find out why the two men seemed to despise each other.

Once again, she was shaken out of her reminiscing stupor. This time she was aroused by the barking of their three large dogs, Shadow, Max and Muffin.

CHAPTER 5

—×—

Hospice Comes To Her Aid

She went to the front door, opened it and waved to the Hospice CNA that was walking through the gate. She thought about how six months ago she refused to allow the doctor to prescribe Hospice. To her it would be giving up on her husband and she wanted to take care of him herself. Finally, in September 2009 she gave in and allowed the doctor to prescribe Hospice. He had been in the hospital four times since moving to Arizona. One week after his fourth time in the hospital, he had a doctor's appointment. Upon getting home, he was exhausted. After a week, Selia called to cancel his next appointment and requested Hospice help. He would continually put off bathing because it was so difficult for him and she found it more difficult every day to take care of his needs. She was afraid to go to the grocery store because she would have to leave him alone. This was extremely worrisome to her.

She just realized her memory lane episodes skipped from 1992 to 2009. She did not want to leave out the important parts of their life together. She vowed to herself to go back and remember their life together before he passes and not miss a moment, even if they were not in order.

Now that Hospice was involved in their lives she was relieved of the hard work of bathing him. Once the doctor called in Hospice, everything went very fast. The intake person was out the next day and by that afternoon a hospital bed, table and other necessities were delivered to the house.

The next day the Hospice RN and CNA came over and a schedule was developed that fast. The CNA would be over every Monday, Wednesday and Friday and the RN would be over every Tuesday and Thursday. She later learned the normal schedule for Hospice visits only included one, maybe two days a week for the CNA and 1 day a week for the RN. He still had it. His swagger and confidence did not leave him even during his dying period. He told them what he wanted and they did what he said. They also assigned a volunteer to come over once a week so Selia could leave the house for a few hours without worrying. She actually just used that time to go grocery shopping. Selia requested a volunteer who liked to bake cookies. She loved to cook but hated to bake so James could have his favorite cookies that he used to bake.

She began calling the people who came into her home "Angels." They were only there about an hour each time (except for the volunteer). That was an hour a day she had just for herself. She would go outside at that time and just walk around the property or go to her computer to play spider solitaire. Doing that gave the "Angels" the freedom to develop a relationship with their patient. He looked forward to their visits every day because he now had someone new to talk to. He enjoyed telling his life stories to them. He never talked about his past with anybody but Selia so the fact that he was now describing his past presented a worry for her.

As the months went by, James's stories became more vivid. These are the stories that only his wife knew. He never told them to anybody so his past would stay as far away as possible. The "Angels" started relating to her that he was telling some very wild stories and thought he had quite an imagination. She listened to their recap of his stories and verified for the "Angels" that he was not hallucinating and that he, indeed, did have the colorful past that he described. She worried that his trips down memory lane could be a bad sign. Was he actually verbalizing "his life flashing before his eyes" or did he just want his life to have mattered. Well, James's life did matter a whole bunch to Selia.

One night Selia woke up to a crashing sound. Even though James was in a hospital bed, the master bedroom was incredibly large. Selia slept in their bed and James's bed was at the front of the bedroom where the television and sitting area existed. She woke with a start and ran to James's bed. He was awake at that point. He explained that he was having a bad dream about his younger days. He said he was in a shabby motel with some bad guys holding a gun to him and all he wanted to do was get out of the room. In his dream, he picked up something large, and threw it at the window so he could then jump out the window and attempt to get away. Selia calmed him down and saw that he was able to go back to sleep. She did not tell him until the next day what actually happened.

The next morning James asked her to sit down next to him in the bed. He was very serious about his request. He looked Selia in the eyes with fear in his own eyes. This was the first time she had seen that look ever. He seriously asked, "Are you dealing drugs?" In order to lighten the mood, Selia said "Of Course. Who do you think is feeding you the morphine and all kinds of other drugs."

This is when Selia explained to him what happened the night before. He had no recollection of any of it. She explained to him he had picked up the shot glass that was on his bed table and threw it. The heavy bottom glass shot glass hit the bottom corner of the television set and left a hole in the screen. Crazily, it did not affect the television screen at all even though it had a hole in it. At that point, James started to recall his dream. He expressed how sorry he was it happened. Once again, James was not concerned about himself. He was only concerned about his bride and any trouble he may have caused.

She was just reminded of the fact James was the first person in her life that was not a controlling or jealous type of person. The proof of this personality trait he had was when they met in Petaluma after work one day. They got a room for two nights because they were attending a wedding the next day and decided not to drive home after the wedding until the next day. Once settled into their room they went down to the bar and restaurant. While sitting at the bar, Selia was talking to a young man who was telling her how he took the bus every Friday to the bar because it was karaoke night. He talked about how sometimes he does not get his chance to sing a song because he is always there and he hoped he could sing that night. He was finally called to be the next singer and was extremely happy. He chose a popular love song to sing. While singing he performed the song directly at Selia. He actually walked as close to her as possible while singing and never took his eyes off her. When he came back to his bar stool, James told him his song was very good and wanted to buy him a drink to thank him. If James had been her first husband, he would have gotten up off his bar stool, punched the poor young man in the face and accused Selia of knowing the young man before that night. The second husband would have just grabbed her and guided her out the door.

CHAPTER 6

—×—

More In The Romance Of

Another day dawns and the process starts all over. She fixes him a simple breakfast, gives him his morning pills, visits, chats with him for a while, and then settles him back into bed. Ten to twenty minutes of visiting is about all he can handle before he is too out of breath to chat anymore.

After finding out that James was reliving his life through his stories to the "Angels," she felt compelled to finish her own walk down memory lane before he passed on. She was now proficient at puttzing around the house and taking her trip down memory lane at the same time. While cleaning up the kitchen, her mind wandered back to Sam's Club where they had met.

It was one week before Christmas. While sitting at the corner bar stools, James presented her with a small box with a beautiful bow on it. She felt embarrassed to receive it. While she loved every minute they spent together, she was worried things were going way to fast. In the box she found a pair of round cut, blue Topaz stud earrings. James told her he bought them because the soft blue color reminded him of her eyes. She went around the corner to the ladies room, removed her earrings and put in the gifted studs. He seemed so proud of himself she didn't have the guts to say anything other than how much she loved the earrings. She didn't want him to know that she had a square cut pair of studs that were a smoke blue color that she loved.

One of the regulars at Sam's Club went over to them and invited them to a New Year's Eve party at his house. We looked at each other and both said we would love to attend.

James made hotel reservations for the night. He worked that day and she met him at the hotel donning the hottest dress he had ever seen. He complimented her over and over again. He said that this would be her night not to worry about drinking too much because he would be the designated driver.

The party was at a home in the Marina County Club. She watched James interact with all the people they had just met. Again, she could see there was something special about him. It appeared all the women at the party found him quite handsome and easy to talk with. He was charming and smooth. Selia was not the jealous type and loved watching the other women making a fuss over him.

The rest of the night at the hotel was great as usual. Now that they had been sleeping together almost two months, they settled into the comfort of familiarity. There was one thing that bothered her. Instead of his arm around her all night, he now hugged a pillow. She felt stupid but found she was jealous of a pillow.

When morning came they talked about how much they both enjoyed being together and how much fun the previous night party was. She decided it was time he found out where she lived. This is when he brought up his past. He explained that his life and work in New York was not always on the up and up and repercussions from his past could possibly follow him to California. He said he did not want her to continue the relationship and go to her house if she was worried about his past. She remembers rolling her eyes at his comments and thinking he was being dramatic. Selia thought for a few moments. This mysterious man intrigued her. Her thoughts went back to her high school years and her mother hood years when her children were young. Everyone she knew considered her "a goody-goody." She remembered that she always followed the social norms of what society expected of her. She quickly decided she wanted to take a walk on the wild side and not care about what other people thought of her.

He followed her home to the little town in the next county called Costner where she owned a duplex and lived in the front half of it. Her daughter and grandson lived in the back half. At this point, her memory lane trip gets a little foggy. She recalls they were together every day from that day on, but how it actually happened is not clear to her after 17 years of 24/7 togetherness. She remembers going to Contra Costa County the next day where he lived in a small cottage on his mother's property where they gathered his belongings (as meager as they were), visited with his mother and left to begin their life together.

This is where she found out why he called her Selia. It was his mother's name and it came very easy to him. She thought it was quite a coincidence. She did not know anybody else with the same name.

While visiting with James's mother, she grilled Selia. Selia was determined to have a good relationship with James's mother, unlike her relationship with her second mother-in-law who she actually kicked out of her house one time and told her to never come back.

Much later in the couples' relationship, James's mother was in her mood of being mad at one of her children. This time she was upset with James and we never figured out why. She was talking to Selia in front of James disparagingly. After some time, Selia could not listen to her anymore. She stood up, pointed her finger at James's mother and shouted at her "that is my husband you are talking nonsense about and because we are joined at the hip, you are disparaging me as well." Selia walked out the door and never went to see his mother again. James followed shortly after. Of course, James continued his relationship with his mother as Selia expected and urged him to. James was not one bit upset that Selia never saw his mother again.

This incident was much later in their relationship. Prior to that incident Selia did everything she possibly could to make her mother-in-law happy and spent as much time with her as she could.

—×—

CHAPTER 7

Life Begins Together And "What Is A Wise Guy?"

What a beginning of life together it was. It was obvious from the get-go the two men in her life (James and her 22-year-old son) were not going to get along. They did not come together as a family. She and James worked all day, while the son slept. At night, they would go to the bedroom to watch television while the son went out and partied.

Weekends for the lovers were spent going to places she had never been before or revisiting areas they both liked. Often they went North up the coast, taking pictures of broken down country fences that James liked. James called them "brandy trips" because there was always a bottle of brandy in the trunk. Stops along the way would be to sit and view the sunset while sipping on brandy or watching the seals at the mouth of the Russian River where it met the Pacific. They just had a lot of laid-back togetherness.

One Saturday morning he said he was going to take her to breakfast where the parking lot is in the middle of the road in the delta area. She had never been to the delta and actually did not know what a delta was. This was the beginning of new adventures for the two of them.

The delta trips included photos of windmills and the ferryboats that would take cars from one side of the delta to the other. The ferryboat was the only way to get to the road that would take you home.

It was a Monday morning and she was walking from the bedroom to the bathroom to shower and get ready for work. She heard a scream from the bedroom "Oh no, not Janet Reno." She ran back into the bedroom and asked what he was screaming about. He pointed to the television and said her. President Clinton just appointed her Attorney General. He explained that she was the New York County District Attorney and had indicted him three times while he lived in New York County, and she lost all three times. He said that the last words Janet Reno ever said to him were, "Someday I will get you James."

Of course, she asked what the hell he was talking about and what did he get indicted for. His explanation came in a very vague manner. He said for the 20 plus years he lived in New York he made his living as a wise guy; which meant that his income was not made in a legitimate or legal way. She had no idea what a wise guy was before this and did not want to go into what he actually did when he lived in New York. All of it would come out eventually, as she would find out down the road.

Since he moved in and changed his mailing address his personal mail started coming to the home they shared. There was not much but one thing of importance arrived. Back in the old days, the Social Security Administration mailed a yearly statement to everybody over 50 showing their reported income for the last 20 years and how much their social security income would be IF. When Selia saw this document, the reality of James's statement that he made his living in non-legitimate ways came to life. There was 20 years of dates and total amount of reportable income for each of those 20 years was ZERO.

Once again, she was brought out of her memory lane experience by the barking of the dogs. The oxygen deliveryman, Joel, from Downtown Drugstore was making his twice-monthly visit to check on the oxygenator machine and deliver some portable tanks. James always loved it when he arrived because he was the only male healthcare person that came to the house. Even though he was confined to a hospital bed, his dry sense of humor still showed through.

Joel was never at the house for very long. His job was to make sure the oxygen equipment was working correctly and to replace any portable tanks that were used up as needed. He always seemed a little irritated when James wanted to keep him talking, but, thankfully, James never saw it that way.

She walked Joel to the door, said thank you and good-bye and went back to James. She took care of his needs, patted him, kissed his cheek and wished this would all be over and done. Many people misunderstood her exclamations of wishing he would die. The doctor said he would probably live about six months and watching him deteriorate so quickly was horrifying. She so hated watching him suffer. His impending death is not what she wanted to dwell on right now – it was the incredible life spent together that mattered to her and her desire to go through it all before the end arrives.

—×—

CHAPTER 8

New Adventures In The Delta

Now that she saw James was nourished and made comfortable, she settled into her trip down memory lane again while working on her kitchen-remodeling project. This project kept her near the master bedroom and her hands busy. There were some who thought she was a little daft using mastic to put one large Mexican beach rock at a time on the kitchen wall around the baking center, the pantry, the laundry room door and all around to the cupboards on the other side of the kitchen.

Every now and then, a rock that was supposed to be stuck to the wall would fall and make a loud bang on the floor. James would shout out to Selia asking if she was okay. Selia new James got a kick out of what she was doing. She even took all the cupboard doors off, made new ones out of tongue and groove knotty pine and trimmed around the ceiling to tie it all together. When it was completed, that end of the kitchen looked like a wine cellar.

As she got busy with her rocks, she thought back to when he took her to breakfast at the Delta when they first started living together. He was right. The parking lot for the café was in the middle of the street. While they ate breakfast, he started telling her about his adventures in the delta area. His grandfather was a prominent person in Contra Costa County and lived on Mare Island. He always went fishing with his grandfather so he could drive him home on the boat when grandpa passed out from too much alcohol. Apparently, grandpa was quite a drinker because he also kept an apartment in the city where he worked for the after work hours when he drank too much to drive home to Mare Island.

He laughed when he told her about when his mother would be bringing up groceries to their apartment on the second floor, drop a bag and hear glass break at which time she would say "Please, let it be the milk." He talked about how he did not know his mother until he was about 11 years old because his father kidnapped him and his sister and took them to live in another state with his paternal grandparents. He commented he was in the schoolyard one day and a beautiful woman came up to the fence and said hello, I am your mother. Do you want to come with me? He jumped the fence and left. They worked for many weeks and finally got the sister back to California. Through the months before the two of them getting married, she would hear a lot about his twisted life. The story James related about his mother was crazy. He explained his mother had been a concert pianist, had an affair and became pregnant. That is when his father took his two young children to another state to live with their grandparents.

When the children were reunited with their mother, they met their half-brother named Charles. James and Charles became very close. Even when they became adults, they continued their close relationship. Apparently, both James and Charles were quite good at playing pool. Charles was married and had a nine-month-old baby girl. James in his car and Charles, his wife and baby in their car headed to Las Vegas. James and Charles were entered in a pool contest that had a large purse for the winner. All of a sudden, there was a head on collision a few cars in front of James. When he was ready to pass the accident, he saw that it was his brother's car. The entire family in the car died and James never played pool again.

After breakfast, they put the top down on the Spider and he drove her around the delta area stopping at all the little "dives." If they had one drink at the dive, it meant they would not need to go back ever again. If they had two drinks, it was "a keeper" on the list of fun places to frequent. This was their first trip to the delta area together so they really over-did everything. She loved the area from the minute they crossed over the Vista Bridge. It had an ethereal quality to it and made her feel like she just drove into a

European village. What they expected to be their last stop before heading home ended up being their downfall. They stopped at the Hotel Rio for their last drink or two and realized they had way too much to drink all day and decided to spend the night at the hotel. The bartender said there was a room available and handed them a key. They both giggled because it appeared they rented rooms by the hour by the way the bartender asked how long they wanted to use it.

James explained how people from all over the delta area would cross over the river to eat prime rib at the Hotel. They ate a great prime rib dinner, danced to the live band and slept like babies cuddled together in the small, tastefully decorated room.

It was not long after their first trip to the delta area that James's tumultuous past showed up. James continually complained that the doors to the house were never locked. She finally agreed to make sure they were locked at night when they were asleep, but did not care about the rest of the time because she had lived in the cute little duplex for over 10 years and never locked the doors before. She was determined not to change her way of doing things and saw it as another means of antagonizing her son. After all, James was the one who moved in with her.

James finally realized, because of her stubbornness, he had to tell her why he was so insistent about the doors being locked. He explained he received a phone call from his ex-partner in New York to warn him that Billy was on his way to California with the intention of doing great bodily harm to him. The reason was Billie blamed James for his brother's death in prison. When she asked him about it, he admitted he had taken care of the business end of his death and assured her that no one was ever murdered who did not deserve it.

She rolled her eyes thinking he was being dramatic again and then consented to the door locking adventure.

As the weeks went by, he would ask her every weekend what she wanted to do and her answer was always "go to the delta." She loved the rustic charm of the area and all the waterways. Whenever there was a festival, they would be there, especially the Crawdad Festival. He loved the delta area also, not just for his childhood memories of fishing with his grandfather, but for the "12" he received on the way to a festival at Bridge Tower for which he had to pull off the road. The little Fiat was also becoming one of his favorite places to be. He talked about that "12" experience often for the next 17 years, all the way up to the time he died. It soon became an every weekend affair to travel to the delta area so they started making reservations at the bed and breakfast in a tiny town in the delta area called "The Inn at the Delta."

After a few weeks, James informed her that the worry about Billy coming to do "great bodily harm" was over but he still preferred to continue to keep the doors locked.

She asked how he knew it was true. Again, his response was his ex-father-in-law called him to say that Billy was found in the Taos, New Mexico; had been involved in a hit and run as a pedestrian and the driver backed up over his legs after knocking him down. This was the plan the ex-partner had set up. Not to kill him, just send him a message.

Selia wondered, so she called the local newspaper. She asked if there was an article recently published about the incident and what was the name of the victim. The responder on the other end of the phone gasped, told her the name of the victim and hurriedly asked what she knew about the incident. She immediately hung up.

She finally asked how he got into the business of being a "wise guy." His explanation was very simple. He was managing bar tender at a casino in Las Vegas on Fremont Street in the early 60's. A beautiful young woman kept frequenting his bar when he was bartending. She visited James at his bar and reported she was going home, back to New York, and asked him to follow her there. He did just that. Hmm, is there a pattern of behavior starting to appear? The beautiful young woman's father just happened to be the "Don" and James's new life business began.

As each day went by, they became closer and closer. They had been living together for 2 months and neither of them could imagine not being together forever. They both worked in Marin County and met for lunch many times. When Selia had public night meetings she would look up and he would be in the audience, give him a quick smile, and go back to engaging in the meeting.

James often commented that he wished they had met 30 years earlier. He would always say what beautiful children they would have had. Selia always responded it would not have worked. She knew she was not the same person she was 30 years ago and her personal growth to the current time is why they loved being together so much. Their relationship was based on total respect for each other, was nothing like either of them had ever experienced and they both wanted it to never end.

CHAPTER 9

Next Step - marriage

Things are going fast now. Not only in their life together, but in his inability to breath. The amount of time she has with him is getting shorter and shorter. She stills has a lot of togetherness to follow down memory lane.

With calendar in hand, they sat up in bed and started with December 7th. Nope, it's Pearl Harbor Day. November, can't because of Thanksgiving. They worked backward and ended on May 7, 1993 for the next step. In the pursuing 4 months, nothing but joy in being together enveloped the two lovers. They continued their weekend trips to the Delta and still enjoyed it immensely. Selia loved how every time they passed the road sign "Soft Shoulder" James would rub her shoulder and softly speak the sign wording.

The "next step" day came and went via a trip to Lake Tahoe. Life together was warm and fuzzy. Then one day she asked him when his birthday was. She should have noticed it on the marriage certificate they both had to sign. Especially since the clerk, performing the ceremony put the wrong date on the license and they had to sign it twice. She was shocked – it was June 5th. June 5th, 1964 was her first date with her children's father; June 5th, 1965 was their marriage date. Years go by and the next bad luck June 5th was the assassination of Bobby Kennedy which just happened to be the first time she was old enough to vote. Back in the 60's a person had to be 21 to vote. Again, years go by, and her son was badly injured at school and had to have immediate surgery on his left elbow – June 5th. Years go by and her daughter had to have immediate surgery on one of her kidneys – June 5th. She started to make sure she stayed home alone on future June 5th's. There were many other incidents of the curse but not significant. Once again, she went to work and told her boss not to make her do anything important. When he asked why, she screamed, "It's June 5th and my garage door fell off its track and landed on my head when I tried to close it."

On their way home from Tahoe, they took, their time stopping in neat little towns acting like tourists. When they arrived at the Delta area, they decided to stay for the night at the Inn at the Delta before going home as husband and wife.

As it turned out, she was very happy she did not know when his birthday was before they got married. She might not have married him. Even though there was one last incident on June 5th, 1993, the curse was lifted and the cursed day turned in to a blessed day from then on.

It just dawned on her how James found out about how stubborn she was and chuckled aloud as she reminisced. When James first moved in with her, he saw her cutting tomatoes for a salad. He immediately pulled out his sharpening steel, moved the blade of a larger knife across the round steel, handed it to Selia and said she was not using a proper knife. She threw it down on the counter and said she preferred her favorite steak knife and left the kitchen. The knife was a 1963 freebee given at the local Chevron for filling up a gas tank. Dinner was completed by James.

She chuckled again. The second time James found out about her stubbornness, it was two days before they were to get married. She told James she thought she would get her hair cut before they went to Tahoe. He busted out with an adamant NO. He said he loved her long, wavy locks and did not want her to cut it. As you can imagine, when she returned home from work the next evening, she was sporting an extremely, short haircut. James giggled and said she looked beautiful.

The amount of time during her daily life workings Selia has to travel down memory lane is getting longer each day, but she knows the length of time she has with him is getting shorter by the day.

CHAPTER 10

——×——

Who's Attle - I Want To See Attle Too

The cute little front unit of her duplex turns out to be a haven for the in love couple. Sunday morning was always a fun morning.

James would get up; make coffee and breakfast. After breakfast, they would go to the deck with a Bloody Mary in hand. The deck was on the front of the duplex over the garage. The driveway across the street was the secondary exit/entrance to and from St Joseph's Catholic Church. As cars would exit from there, because of a slight up tilt of the roadway, the sight line of the people inside the auto was straight up towards the couple sitting on the front deck, both in bathrobes, sipping a Bloody Mary. So many times the driver would flash thumbs up. It soon became a Sunday morning fun game. As cars would come out the exit, they both would hold up their drinks in salute and we continued to get the thumbs up signal from the driver.

It was a cozy place to be. Every morning the front door would crash open and the little guy named Bobby would run in and jump in bed between them. Bobby is Selia's grandson who lived with his mother in the unit in back. This little lad soon became James's favorite person to be around. Easter came around and the two lovers stayed up for hours coloring Easter eggs to hide for an egg hunt for James's favorite little person. All but one egg was found the next morning.

It was the next-door neighbor's birthday so the couple threw a barbeque in his honor. That day the mail carrier delivered a wedding invitation to James's nieces wedding. James was telling the neighbor about going to Seattle in August. Bobby ran up to his gramma and said "Gramma, who's Attle, I want to see Attle too."

The day of flying out to Seattle would be a day Selia never would forget. She took care of the airline and B&B they would be staying at right away. As it turned out, the day they were flying out was her birthday. Every week for 3 months, she would comment to James in a sing/song fashion "We are flying out on my birthday." It became a ritual. He did not seem to pay attention. She just figured it was his usual laid-back attitude but he was planning to surprise her. NOT!

Before going to SFO to fly to Seattle, he said they needed to make a trip to the Delta to go to the bank in Rio Vista. As they had been making weekend trips to the area for months it seemed reasonable. After the banking was done, they crossed the street to one of their favorite dive bars and ordered a Bloody Mary. While sitting at the bar, James, in a very serious manner, asked Selia to remind him on September 8th that the next day was his mother's birthday. Oh boy, he is really setting me up for a surprise is what Selia was thinking. She thought he was pretending to forget that today was her birthday and there would be flowers and champagne at the B & B. NOT!

Her memory again is a little fuzzy. She cannot remember anything of any significance due to James forgetting her birthday, but does remember he never forgot again. Selia's mother made a surprise visit. She was dying to meet this third son-in-law. After introductions were made, James asked his new mother-in-law if she would like a glass of wine or something else to drink. She said no because she is dieting to lose weight right now. Selia was in the living room and was mortified when she heard James respond with the statement "I have always heard the best way to lose weight is just don't put food in your mouth."

CHAPTER 11

—— × ——

The Big Move to the Delta
and House Boat Living

The weekend trips to the Delta continued. Finally, Selia suggested looking at moving to their favorite place to visit.

They started looking for boats for sale in the Yachting Magazine. They found a cute 34' Nautaline houseboat for sale; made the call about it, then went the next weekend to see it. As it turned out, the boat was actually used as a love nest for the married man who owned it and his mistress. After they were taken for a short cruise, the owner agreed to allow them to spend one night on the boat. Selia was very claustrophobic and wanted to make sure she could sleep under the helm area where the double bed was.

The sleeping area was great. Selia called it the "womb" because it was so cozy and enveloped the sleeping person. The purchase too place and moving plans began. Selia agreed to live in the boat at its current location for 3 months. The Marina was extremely beautiful and well taken care of, but she preferred a more rustic atmosphere.

And so, the move to the Delta begins. Garage sales, renting a storage space in the small delta town, farming out antiques and artwork to relatives to enjoy but return to Selia when she moves ashore again. They both quit their jobs, packed both vehicles with their clothes and miscellaneous items and off they went to live in their favorite place, the Delta.

This new adventure started in February 1994. James was off finishing his last job. Selia wanted to do some gardening so she got permission to put large pots with flowers at the entrance of the dock finger their boat was on and plant nasturtium seeds along the levy. A few days go by. She was sitting on the front deck of the boat while looking at the dock box and the post going up to the high roof. She decided to paint a rose vine on the post. After sketching a vine with leaves, roses and a few buds, she takes one, two, and the then the third step taken backwards to admire her work lands her in the icy delta water between the front of the boat and the dock.

It was a cold, windy day and Selia was dressed for the weather in jeans, heavy socks and tennis shoes, with a sweatshirt and a hooded sweatshirt over the top. The wind was blowing the boat around so she had to stay in one corner between the boat and the dock, hanging onto the tie line in the freezing cold water. Because of the weight of the heavy, wet clothes and the limited space to move in, she was not able to pull herself up to the dock. Because it was a weekday, very few people were around. It was a good 30 minutes before someone came down the dock. The neighbor lady, Millie, said hello and asked if she was okay.

Selia quietly said "No." Millie tried to pull her out but due to the weight of the heavy, wet cloths, she was not able to help. Selia told her to go down the dock to Richard's boat. He was also a live aboard. Millie came back shortly and reported that Richard was taking a nap and he would be down in a few minutes. When Richard arrived, he surveyed the situation, told Selia to hold up her left arm, and expect it to hurt a little. He wrapped his large, muscular hands around her left arm. Waited for a gust of wind to push the boat away from the dock to the extent of the rope tie down, and yanked as hard as he could. Selia flew out of the small space she was trapped in and went belly down on the dock.

She jumped up, thanked Richard and ran to the back of the boat. By this time, it was already dark so she stripped all her clothes off and went into the boat from the back door. She did not want to go in the front door with wet clothes on because she was going to hide the incident from James. She grabbed her bathrobe and a towel, which she wrapped around her head and then sat down on the couch. She knew James would be home at any time. Sure enough, she heard him coming down the dock about ten minutes later. He entered and asked, "What's going on." The response was Selia saying, "Oh, nothing, I just took a shower and my hair is still wet" was hysterical. "Oh, really, then why does the finger going all the way to the back of the boat have giant wet puddles on it?"

James laughed and stated he thought that his bride already knew not to take even one footstep backwards when living on a boat. From that day on, Selia continued to do her gardening with paints on the dock box and post, but never took even one-step backwards. The left side of her entire body from her armpit to her ankle was black and blue from the experience. Her gardening became a joy to all the people who docked their boat on the same finger. They would walk by and say I see you are gardening today, looks good. The maintenance man at the Marina would start at the small boat finger and work his way down to the large, 50' and above boat docks painting all the posts and dock boxes. He never painted Selia's dock box or post because he promised her he would not ruin her garden.

Coming out of her trip down memory lane, this time was especially warming to her heart. She was reminded that when he passed she still felt like a bride. Every time he would introduce her to someone, he would say, "I would like you to meet my bride." Whenever he would refer to her in a conversation, he always said "my bride." After 17 years of togetherness, she realized he never stopped referring to her, treating her, looking into her eyes as anything but his bride.

One thought leads to another, and Selia suddenly remembered their trip to the furniture store where they purchased their new leather couch. The couch they brought from California was placed in the living room. The living room was only used when Selia hosted one of her open houses. The television was in the family room and that is where they needed a couch. So, off they went to the furniture store. She knew exactly what she was looking for. They walked through the store many times and could not find what she wanted; was told they did not have any in stock or in the warehouses, so she picked out a regular type couch that could be delivered in about a month. Four months went by and the couch had not arrived, so the two of them drove to the store to inquire. As they were walking around all the furniture, Selia saw exactly what she wanted; a leather curved sectional with a recliner on one end, a pull out double bed in the middle and a chaise on the other end.

They went to the checkout counter and requested the couch that was supposed to have been delivered months ago and already paid for in cash, to be exchanged with the sectional on the floor. The salesperson adamantly stated it could not be done because the couch Selia ordered was a special order. She was okay with the decision but a little disappointed also. They left the store and after about 2 miles down the road, James made a big U-turn and told his bride she would get what she wanted.

They drove back to the store and James walked in with his slow moving steps and straight upright posture to the same salesperson at the checkout counter. Selia was right behind him. James looked at the salesperson and said in his soft spoken but firm voice, "Young man, my bride is not happy and you are going to make sure she is happy, right?" The young man stuttered a bit and then said the new couch was about $1,000 more and he would not write up the sale until they went home and measured to see that it would fit. Selia told the young man it would fit and they would pay the extra money at that time. The salesperson wrote up the new sales slip with the exchange but he would not authorize the delivery until they went home and measured. They went home, Selia walked directly to the telephone and called the salesperson and told him it would fit, the couch was delivered that afternoon. The Bride was extremely happy, not only did the couch fit; it fit so good it looked like it was specially made for the space.

Selia had never seen James's eyes and expression directed at other people when he was in that bad boy mode. She wished she had been in a better position so she could see what they looked like. She had only seen his loving eyes.

—×—

CHAPTER 12

Life on the Delta is good
– Oh Oh, watch out

The usual hoopla is going on. CNA and/or RN are at the house looking after James and Selia begins her memory lane trip again while working on her rock walls.

They moved to the Delta the next February after getting married in May, 1993. It was mother's day when Selia saw her daughter and her boyfriend and grandson Bobby coming down the dock. What a wonderful surprise. James and Selia decided to take their guests out for a ride in the boat. Everyone was assigned a life jacket, including Schotzee, James and Selia's Schnauzer. He was put in his jacket and he looked so cute sitting at the screen door watching the water pass by.

It was a beautiful, sunny day and the wind was minimal. The Delta area is known for its late afternoon winds. This would be the first time since moving onto the boat that James was actually taking it out for a spin. Selia was not one bit worried, as she knew James was an experienced boater.

It was so exiting. Watching the levy walls go by. The delta waters were much more beautiful when actually down inside the levy. When on the levy road it was not as beautiful as actually being in the waterway. After boating along the waterways for about an hour, James decided it was time to go back to the marina before the delta winds came up. When they bought the boat, the owner warned them about trying to get the boat into the dock slip when the wind was up.

Captain James made a wide turn near the Tower Bridge so they could begin their trip back to the marina. As they were getting closer to the marina, the wind came up. Turning into the marina was difficult and then once turned into the waterway between slip fingers the small boat suddenly became the Queen Mary. James had been told by the previous owner, a houseboat will suddenly become like a kite and the winds blow it around mercilessly. Well, the Queen Mary hit a boat on the opposite side of the waterway, then hit the boat in the directly beside slip and ripped apart the back deck railing from the boat the couple called home. After much forward, backward motion to get the boat into the slip, it finally happened. James shouted instructions to all aboard – jump off and get it tied off before he turned off the engine, fix a drink for him. Selia went directly to the galley to fix drinks. The boyfriend jumped off, put the bumpers down and tied the boat to the dock.

Once all that was done, everybody was ready for a cocktail to calm the nerves. At that point, James looks at Selia and commences his diatribe about being the First Mate she was supposed to get the boat tied off before fixing drinks. Everybody laughed at him. Fortunately, the boyfriend was a welder. They unscrewed the entire back railing so he could take it home and weld the sections back together. The other two boats were repaired at James and Selia's expense.

After their first boating trip in their HOME that contained everything they owned, the couple decided NEVER to take their home and everything they owned out of the slip it lived in. They soon bought a dingy so they could travel the waterways without putting their home in jeopardy. They named the boat "The Bobby" so when Bobby came to visit, Grampa could teach him how to travel the waterways in his own boat. Grampa's favorite person came to visit often and everybody loved the time spent together.

One of the things Selia loved about living on the boat was all week long the marina and especially their dock was deserted except for two other boats that were live aboard boats. Consequently, it felt like the long dock was all theirs. On weekends, the marina was crawling with people but the only sounds heard were happy sounds. The sounds were of people enjoying themselves. It was always fun on the weekends to turn the radio on and listen to people out on the waterways calling for a tow because they went aground and all kinds of crazy events but nothing ever seriously wrong.

Time has gone by, they celebrated their first wedding anniversary and finding a job seems impossible. Any time she wanted a new job, Selia always had a good job within days. She thought it just had to be the economic times. Things got so tight that both James and Selia took minimum wage jobs in the Delta. At that time minimum wage was $5.25 an hour. Both had worked professional jobs in the past and would have been embarrassed to work for minimum wage, but loved the Delta so much it was worth the struggle. James went to work at Bluto's Marina as the breakfast and lunch line cook. It was a bar, restaurant and marina. Selia went to work at the Inn in the Delta where they used to stay when they were in the area. She worked Friday, Saturday and Sunday checking people in and out at the Inn.

They did not need much, just enough to pay the boat slip monthly, which included the electricity and water. Selia started collecting aluminum cans from other people who docked their boats at the marina. James did not want her to do that because of his pride. The cans actually put them over the top in order to eat and buy cigarettes and booze. A carton of cigarettes at that time was $7.00.

One late afternoon, James arrived home to the cute little love nest they shared. He was shaking so bad Selia got frightened. He choked out that he had seen a ghost from his past while at work. She fixed him a cocktail in order to calm him down. After a bit, he was able to talk about it.

He explained he left the kitchen to go to the men's room. This meant he had to go through the dining room. He saw a man sitting at a table by the window having coffee and reading the newspaper. They both stared at each other but didn't say a word. He explained it was his best friend from New York named Rudy. He had been told by the FBI that Rudy was making a drug run to the Bahamas in James's large Mathews wooden boat when it was blown up and Rudy died. James said he has never stopped mourning the death of his best friend and was in shock that he was still alive.

Selia tried to console James and convince him that it really was just someone who looked like Rudy. James was adamant about it actually being Rudy because nobody holds a newspaper the way Rudy did.

A few weeks later, they were reading the local newspaper. There was a large article about a recent drug bust in the Delta naming all the people who were arrested. One name was "Rudy." That is when James convinced Selia it was his best friend who obviously had been in the witness protection program through the FBI and had decided to go his own way.

When the two of them flew to Seattle to his nieces wedding, Selia met his sister. The only thing the sister talked about was how hard she worked to lose weight before her daughter's wedding. Selia was not impressed and could not believe they were brother and sister.. The sister called and informed James she and her husband were taking a road trip to Los Angeles to see their son and planned to stop by to visit us on the boat. This visit would be the beginning of the end for Selia having a relationship with her new sister-in-law.

They arrived early afternoon for a short visit. The sister was not one bit impressed with the cute love nest they chose to call home. The first thing she wanted to do was see the dock where the large 50' and larger boats were. Selia kindly offered to take her down to the large boat dock. As they were walking down the dock where they lived, the sister boldly stated that she was embarrassed to introduce her brother to anybody because of his gray hair and reported that she brought him a box of Grecian Formula for men so he could dye his hair.

A wave of shock came over Selia and she came to a dead stop. Her mind was reeling about how this woman could be embarrassed when her appearance was such that it was obvious she worked very hard to put all the weight she lost for her daughter's wedding back on plus an extra 100 pounds. In order to keep peace, she did not verbalize her disgust for the obese woman.

James finally convinced the visitors they should be getting down the road before it got too late. After they left, Selia told James what she thought of his sister and her ridiculous comments. She then took the box of Grecian Formula and threw it in the garbage. James laughed but got the message loud and clear. He never seemed to get upset with his bride. He later explained that he has always protected his sister because she had a brain tumor a long time ago and when it was removed, she had lost many essential brain cells.

CHAPTER 13

—✕—

Open House Boat Party

Time seems to be moving slowly. Selia had many interviews but nothing ever came of them. Because living in the Delta was very close to Contra Costa County, the couple often visited James's mother. Her new mother-in-law seemed to be enamored with her daughter-in-law. It did not take long before she showed her true self. She showed Selia many photos and it seemed the photos always appeared to be torn in half. Apparently, every time she got mad at one of her children, she would go through photos and tear them in half to remove the disgraced sibling.

The mother-in-law and Uncle Joe lived in the same house, owned a lot of property together in Contra Costa and were business partners. Uncle Joe was the husband of the deceased sister of Selia's new mother-in-law. Prior to the sister passing, an agreement was made that Selia (the mother-in-law) would take care of Uncle Joe.

It was getting close to Thanksgiving and Christmas. Selia helped her mother-in-law deliver turkeys and hams to each of her tenants. There were many tenants as Uncle Joe and she owned many, many rental units. This was when Selia discovered her mother-in-law put up a gruff, mean face all the time, but really was a very kindhearted person.

She also gave to James and Selia a large turkey and a ham. In Selia's previous life, she put on a Christmas Eve open house for many, many years. Each year it grew bigger and bigger. This made her want to have "open house boat" for the holidays. They decided on December 10th for their first event. As it turned out, it also happened to be the same day as the lighted boat parade.

With borrowed barbeques, the turkey and ham were roasted. Selia made many types of finger foods and salads, bought booze and the party was on. The marina was full of people all week with people decorating their boats for the parade. Selia walked around all week informing people of the open house boat. On the day of the party, she would holler across the waterway wherever she saw people and told them to come over and eat. The maintenance man at the marina brought down two large folding tables for the food. These tables sat on the dock at the front of the decorated houseboat that was the love nest. Guests began to arrive. She saw her mother coming down the dock with a tall, handsome young man and wondered where she picked him up. She did not recognize the young man until they got right in front of her. She screamed and hugged the young man. It was her son. She had not seen him for two years and the last time she saw him he had shoulder length hair. He now had a buzz cut and a scruffy stubble beard. She was embarrassed that she did not recognize him but happy he was there. What a success it was. Selia was extremely happy and informed James they would be doing open house boat every year as long as they lived there. The lighted boat parade was beautiful and the winning decorated boat just happened to belong to Richard who pulled Selia out of the drink.

Both James and Selia loved living on the boat. The simplicity of the life style was why it was so enjoyable. One of James's favorite things to do was sitting on the back deck. He would put a piece of dog food on the table not to near him. The area had many scrub blue jays. James would sit very still; a bird would swoop down and pick up the dog food. Each time James would do this, he put the tidbit closer to him. Eventually, the birds were not one bit afraid of him, started landing on his hand, and took their treat.

—✕—

CHAPTER 14

The Good, The Bad and The Ugly

The New Year has begun and still no jobs on the horizon. They both were still working their minimum wage job that has kept them a float, literally. Selia's last interview was in November. Finally, in February the good started. Selia received a call and was offered the job as Deputy City Clerk for the city of Suisun that she accepted immediately. After all the pre-employment hoopla, she began work March 1st. It did not take long to realize she knew more about what the job entailed and how to do it than her boss did. She was hired based on her knowledge and experience in the discipline of governmental workings. It eventually became an ugly situation to deal with.

It was late March when James received a call from his first wife. They had been married when James was about 18 years old and had a child. He loved his son and was very proud of him, but knew he had not been the father his son really needed. She called to let James know that his son had been found dead at his house. It was ruled a suicide, but we found out at the funeral what really happened.

Selia comes out of her memory lane trip at this point. This was so very, very hard for James to deal with. She needs a break from the memory that hurt him so badly, but knows she will have to get back to it eventually.

The CNA leaves after bathing James, changing his bed sheets and just visiting with him. Selia was always amazed how this can happen without taking the patient out of the bed. The Angels know how to do it!

After the "Angel" was gone, Selia went in to visit with James. He talked about how nice his CNA was and how he enjoyed talking with her. Selia took care of making sure he was feed, drank plenty of water, had his medication and settled down for a nap. After every visit from the CNA he was extremely drained of energy.

CHAPTER 15

—— × ——

New Job, New Boss, New Life - AGAIN

This gave her the time to go back into memory lane. She did not want to. It was the hardest point in their married life and she hated having to relive the pain. They had not even been married two years yet. Their second anniversary would not be until May. The funeral was set for early April in Palm Springs. This meant a one-day drive down to Palm Springs; another day back from Palm Springs, funeral attendance, etc. so Selia told her boss that she was going to have to take the next week off to attend the funeral.

All hell broke loose in the office at that point. The City Clerk scolded her new Deputy and hysterically shouted she could not take the time off as she had not been on the job long enough to have the time on the books. Selia in rebuttal exclaimed that her husband was in no shape to make the trip on his own and she would not be in next week. She continued with she didn't care if she didn't get paid for that time off or if she got fired. This was the beginning of three years of total, extreme harassment from her boss.

The rest of that week, Selia did not know what she would find when she got home from work. Her husband had gone into a deep depression, was going through all the "would a, should a, could a, for his son's entire life, and drinking to MORE than excess. The drive to Palm Springs was excruciating. James was sick and shaking the entire trip. Every so often, they had to pull over to the side of the road, Selia would go to the trunk, pour out a shot of brandy and give it to James so he could stop shaking for a bit. The couple had always been people who enjoyed having cocktails together, but Selia had never seen him drink to excess as he was doing at that point.

Upon arriving in Palm Springs, they went through the drive-thru of an In and Out Burger. There were no such burger joints in Northern California so she was looking forward to trying it. Besides, James was in no shape to go into a restaurant. The motel Selia made reservations for was just around the corner. After eating, James's nephew and a few other people came by their room. The reminiscing began and James was surprisingly capable of participating.

Phillip, the nephew, started relating a story of spending a summer with his Uncle James in New York. He expressed his gratitude how his Uncle had paid for getting his teeth fixed, including braces which James continued to pay for the care after Phillip went back home to Oregon. His next story took Selia by surprise. Phillip related, when his Uncle wasn't home, someone knocked on the front door. Phillip opened it and told the man standing there his Uncle was not home. The man proceeded to thrust a garbage bag into Phillip's arms and told him to give it to his Uncle. Like any 13 year old, Phillip opened the top of the bag and discovered it was overflowing with hundred dollar bills. Again, Selia was getting the idea of how a "wise guy" made his living and why his social security statement had nothing but yearly zeros on it.

The funeral was in the morning. It was the first time he had seen his son's mother in over 20 years. Their son was only 27 years old when he passed. Surprisingly, when James was not drinking too much and only thinking of his hurt, he was able to be articulate and participate fully. There were several men of James, Jr's age at the funeral. Most of them tried very hard to avoid getting near the deceased's father. Two of them finally came up to James and Selia, to express their sorrow. James did not believe his son would commit suicide by hanging himself with a belt, so he began pressing the two young men for answers. They did not want to relate anything, but finally said they would if James promised not to go any further with another investigation.

The two young men finally came through. They explained they were having a party, drinking and decided to try the erotic, choking method of having arousal and climax. That was quite a blow. Obviously, losing a 27-year-old son in that manner was excruciatingly painful. James and Selia gasped, thanked the young men and walked away. Neither of them was capable of further discussion at that point.

As things wore down, James went to his son's mother again, comforted her and was happy she did not know the reality of her son's death. She asked for help in paying for the funeral and James promised her he would. Obviously, the couple was living on about $500 a month, Selia had been on her job for less than a month and facing possibly being fired, and they had no cash assets. When they returned to the Bay area, James asked his mother and she was more than happy to help. She loved her grandson. He was an exact twin of his father.

The ride back to the Bay area was similar to the ride down. It seems, when left to just his own thoughts, James would lose control and sink deeper into depression.

Selia returned to work on Monday and did not know what she would be walking into. As luck would have it, her boss was bitter but did not have her fired. She just did not allow her to receive pay for the 5 days she was gone.

As it turned out, Selia's boss decided to send her to a city clerk seminar in Pasadena. She was not happy to go because she was worried about her husband but she did not dare say that to the boss. While at the three-day seminar an unusual coincidence happened. Selia was asked to stand up, introduce herself and where she was from before answering a question. About 30 minutes later a break was called for and Selia went outside to smoke a cigarette. A young, black woman from the City of Calamar approached Selia, introduced herself and stated her ex-roommate and best friend was James and wanted to know if we were related. With surprise in her voice, Selia answered that it was her husband's son and asked the beautiful young woman if she knew that he had passed. She asked how James's father was handling his son's death. When the young woman heard how her best friend's father was dealing with the situation she was extremely upset, ran back into the meeting room, grabbed her purse and left.

When the break was over, the seminar facilitator approached Selia, stated he saw what happened outside and asked about it. Selia repeated what happened and the seminar facilitator was just as astonished about the coincidence of the two of them meeting as she was. He asked if the young woman was coming back and Selia responded with a shrug of "I don't know."

The next morning the young woman did come back to the seminar and came up to Selia and hugged her. She explained she went home (which was about 2 hours away) so she could get some photos of James to give to his father. Selia graciously accepted the photos and asked if her husband could call her if he felt up to it.

When Selia got home, she found that James had survived because she left prepared meals for him but found that his mental status was no better. He did call the wonderful young lady. They talked often for a month or so and it seemed it did really help James with his pain.

As the month's went by, James's depression seemed to progress into a deep darkness and he was drinking so much Selia didn't know what to expect when she got home from work. He had quit showering or putting on clean clothes. She spent an entire weekend preaching at him. He showered and put on clean clothes. That Monday evening upon returning from work, Selia found him on the front deck of the boat wearing a tie and dress shirt, cut off shorts and so intoxicated he couldn't even talk. She guided him into the boat and down two stairs to the lounge. Put him on the couch, covered him with a blanket and hoped he would pass out, which he did. It became a lonely, sad time in Selia's life. Her job, while financially very good, was something she hated going to every day. When she would return home, she had nobody to talk to about how her job was going because James was mentally not available.

To make matters worse, he received yet another bad phone call. This time the call came from New York. His oldest daughter had been ill for some time and was on some high potency medications. She was found dead in bed from an accidental overdose of medication. What next? Well, the "what next" came in the form of the sister.

James's sister called one afternoon. When he hung up the phone, he was even more distraught than before. He reported that she called to tell him some nasty things she had learned about their mother. Because he was already very depressed, he was not able to relate what the sister had actually said. At that point, Selia picked up the phone, called the sister and chewed her out shamelessly. The sister commented her friends understand she had a brain tumor removed and couldn't help herself at times. Selia responded that even a dim wit had to take responsibility for their actions and she was never to call again. If James wished to talk to her, he would call her.

After no less than seven months of living in a horror movie, Selia, early in the morning before James's drinking started anew, sat him down, picked up a cast iron skillet, held it over his head and scolded him like he had never been scolded. (The skillet was for affect only. She wanted him to realize how serious she was). She told him how sorry she was about his son's and daughter's death, that she did not know how she would be able to life through losing a child, but he was alive and had to get back to living life with his new wife. She threatened, if he did not get help or do something to become one of the living again, she was gone out of his life forever. She insisted he quit drinking altogether, or else.

James tried very hard. He often said he wished he could drink the way his wife did. Whenever she did not want another drink, she just stopped. He promised he would not drink anymore. Selia marked a calendar on that day, as "James promised no more drinking." Three months later, he started drinking again and the calendar was marked as such. This situation went on for four more, three month periods. Each time Selia threatened if he starts drinking again she will leave.

While he was on his no drinking period of time, Selia went to Vista Town and put a deposit on a 2 bedroom apartment to rent on the first of the next month. She knew it would be any time soon that his excessive drinking would start so she wanted to be ready. Sure enough, the time came in December, during the open house boat. This time it was different, he came right out and told his bride he was going to drink at the party. Did he ever. He drank brandy straight. Again, he could not seem to control it. Before the end of the month, Selia told James about the apartment and she would be moving to it the next weekend. He asked why. She pulled out the calendar and pointed out the five different times James broke his promises. He was not one bit phased by the written calendar remarks. Instead, he seemed to be in denial. He was very calm and sweet. He smiled and said he understood because he knew she needed office space since becoming a freelance consultant.

His comment as Selia remembers it, caused her to came out of her memory lane stupor. She realized she had not memorialized leaving her job as Deputy City Clerk; going freelance and how it affected their life together. As this was an important time in their life, she found a quiet place and began her memory lane journey again. At this time, James was doing more sleeping than anything and Selia had a lot of time on her hands to remember things.

Selia's tenure as Deputy City Clerk was almost exactly three years. It was three years of sheer torture. She was now the supervisor over five other women, all of which hated the boss and assumed Selia was another one just like the boss. It took almost an entire year for them to realize they were lucky to have Selia as their supervisor. At that point, the entire office began running like a fine tuned piano. No more squabbles, always willingness to help and fully cooperate with each other and all finally enjoyed coming to work, except for Selia. The work was enjoyable and all the people were very nice to work with except for the boss.

The boss seemed to hate the fact that everything was working well; new systems were put into place that worked 100% better than the systems she put into place. The boss tortured Selia daily because of it and wrote up a disciplinary action a minimum of twice weekly. Selia started to have nightmares every Sunday night that she murdered her boss. When leaving the parking lot one evening she saw her bosses car parked, stopped, and stared at it wishing she had a big knife so she could puncture her tires. This was the point at which Selia knew she had to leave her job. Not having anyone to talk to when she got home made it difficult each morning to go to work. Each day she would take personal items home so when she did leave she would leave nothing behind. She did not know when, but new the end was coming very soon.

Fortunately, it came soon. It was a Friday, an event of harassment happened as the boss started her normal carping and screaming at Selia. The next Monday, Selia was once again presented with a written reprimand that would go into her personnel file. Her personnel file was already over a foot deep. It was 10 minutes to noon when the boss handed Selia the reprimand. She read one sentence, stood up, grabbed her purse, looked at her boss, said "You are sick" then walked out and never went back.

The effect on the lovers' marriage was good. Because the boss had a very bad attendance record so Selia was forced to put in a lot of overtime. This worked out to her having so many overtime hours on the record she continued to get full paychecks from March through August. At this point, her freelance career began paying off along with continuing to receive full paychecks. This put them back on a good financial track.

Hence, that is why James was not upset about her impending move off the boat. In his mind, she needed room for an office.

A month or two before telling James about moving to her own apartment, his sister decided to come to California to stay at their mother's house to help her out since she was very ill and bedridden. As it turned out, the dimwitted sister just put her mother's medications at her bedside so she could take them when she needed to take them. Well, good ole Mom would only take the medications that made her feel good, such as the opioids, instead of the mediation to help her COPD condition.

With Mom in an altered state, the sister had her mother sign on her existing will that she disinherits her son and leaves her entire estate to her daughter. Mom died within two weeks of the sister's arrival. The same day of her mother's death, the sister immediately took her mother's will to an attorney. The attorney explained that the newly hand written section was not valid as her mother was in an altered state and she was the only person in attendance when it was written. This was evidenced by the date that it was signed by Mom and a new witness did not sign it.

Consequently, the funeral was very contentious. At the gravesite, the sister approached James and told him he had to pay her $200 for his share of the flowers. That was the only time his sister actually talked to him, so when the gravesite service was over, he exclaimed to his bride he was not going to the cousin's house for the festivities after the funeral. Instead, the couple went to a bar on Mare Island where his grandfather liked to stop and have a drink. At this point, Selia did not care if he had a few drinks. She knew she would be driving home. She wondered how much more could her husband endure and how would he handle being told his bride was moving out.

CHAPTER 16

Moving Day and Beyond

Unfortunately, the move coincided with the death of James's mother. Luckily, for Selia, the furniture she put in her apartment came from the home of her now deceased mother-in-law.

At this point with nothing but his deep depression on his side, James slipped quickly into doing nothing but drinking, smoking and not eating. That is when Selia started to prepare large meals, freeze it in one-person meal sizes and give them to James. He would come over once a week to pick them up. She could not believe how he looked. He was down to about 140 pounds and looked like he was 90 years old.

Selia received a phone call from a hospital in Solano and was informed by the Hospital that her husband had been brought into the hospital by ambulance for alcohol poisoning. The story related to her was her husband called 911 and then passed out. Because of living on the boat, the marina manager had to be awakened to unlock the dock where the boat was moored. The ambulance then took him to the drunk tank; the drunk tank refused to accept him as he appeared to be close to death; hence he ended up in the hospital. The hospital informed Selia her husband was very close to death and if he had not been transported when he was he would have died. The doctor notes relayed if he had not gotten to the hospital when he did, he would have died within 45 minutes. When he was conscious, they asked him about health insurance. James had told them he did not have any so the hospital got him on Medi-Cal so they could be paid for their services. Selia explained there was insurance through her employer, which eventually paid the bill 100%.

James was in the hospital for five days then released with all the information he needed so as not to let the situation every happen again. Selia picked him up, returned him to the boat and informed him, if he stayed sober for one year, they could go back together and continue their life together. He worked very hard to do just that. He went to AA and found a sponsor. His sponsor had him going to meetings 4 times a day 7 days a week to start with. James followed everything to the tee. He was convinced he could never drink again. He knew he was not doing this so he could get back with his wife. The incident scared him to the core so he was doing it for himself because he did not want to die, not yet.

Selia continued to make meals and James would come over once a week to pick them up. He finally started looking like the person he used to be. She purposely did not see him more than that. She was adamant about not becoming a babysitter. Suddenly one day the sister called her. The sister was extremely pushy about what Selia intended relative to her brother. Her response was nothing and at this point she was just living her own life without him. The sister went ballistic and insisted she needed to take care of him and what a horrible person she was if she didn't. Selia's response was extreme. She told the sister it was none of her business, James had her credit card and his mother's old car so if he can drive to the store to get booze and cigarettes he could take care of himself and never call her again then hung up the phone. This statement had many expletives included as Selia figured it was the only way to get through to the dimwitted sister. She did not feel it was any of her business that she was actually cooking for him.

As time goes by, Selia can see that James is becoming more and more of himself, which makes her very happy. It is obvious he has not been drinking. They never speak of it but when the one-year mark arrives, they will both know. Friends and family keep telling her to divorce him. No matter how many times she informs the doubters that she loves him very much and will not desert him, they all think she is crazy.

Just as it seems things are becoming smooth, another pop-up situation shows its nasty head. The cousin who was Uncle Sean's stepdaughter found out that he and James's mother had loaned the couple $20,000 during their hard times out of their business account. Since the time Selia had a full time job they were paying it back at $500 a month. The cousin filed a civil law suit to recover that money. Selia had stopped making the payments because it was stipulated, if either one of the business partners died, the loan was forgiven. None of this was in writing, just understood between the partners. Obviously, the cousin grilled her step-dad to find out about the private loan.

This happened at the same time Selia's mother-in-law's property went into probate court. James came over and showed her the lawsuit. They had 30 days to respond. Selia said she would work on the response. James pointed out that the plaintiff attorney was also a cousin. At that point, James and his AA sponsor took care of cleaning, painting, etc. the only rental unit that his mother owned on her own and not with Uncle Sean. It went into escrow very quickly. The proceeds from the sale was a mere $120,000 but could not be dispersed until probate was finished which would take many months.

James went into his bad boy mode once he knew the property had been sold and funds were waiting to be distributed. Selia was never told exactly how it happened and did not even know it happened for many months. James was very good at putting on the charm. He proceeded to go to the title company where the proceeds from the sale of his mother's rental unit were being held in escrow. That's when his overwhelming charm took over. Somehow, he managed to talk the escrow officer into releasing the funds. A check was made out to the sister, the escrow officer actually mailed it to her and a check was made out to James, each for $60,000. Unbelievable, that escrow officer had to have been severely reprimanded and/or fired after doing it.

As far as the civil lawsuit, Selia wrote the response, James filed it with the court and a court date was set several months down the road. James made the appearance on the court date. When the case was over James visited Selia and let her know it was over. He explained the judge asked him who his attorney was. James responded he did not have an attorney because he did not have any money to pay one. The judge asked him who wrote the response and James replied his wife did. At that point, the judge looked at the opposing Attorney and said, "Young man you might want to take lessons from this man's wife as this is the best written brief I have ever read in all his years as a judge." Coincidentally, the cousin's attorney was the same attorney the sister hoped would tell her the new will her mother signed was invalid.

While still in his academy award winning acting role, James was asked about what happened to the proceeds from the probate of his mother's will. James's response was he did not know. All he could remember was he woke up in New York and had no money left. He explained to the Judge, he is an alcoholic, has been attending AA meetings daily and does not know why he went off the wagon. The judge asked for names of some of the AA members that he sees at the meetings. James gave the judge some first names. The Judge asked for last names of the AA members. James then explained that was all he knew of them; after all, it is called Alcoholics Anonymous. After further testifying, James made it very clear to the judge the loan from his mother and uncle had a stipulation that if either one of them passed it did not have to be repaid because the money was coming from their joint business accounts. After further deliberation, the judge ruled in favor of the defendant James. This made the cousin very, very mad and she never talked to James again.

Selia's freelance business was going so well that she was able to put $1,000 a month or more in a savings account. This made her happy because she wanted to buy a house and she could save up a good down payment. Unfortunately, when tax time came around she owed Uncle Sam $12,000 and State of California $800. There went her down payment and she had to sell her sports car to pay the State.

James was doing very well in his sobriety. He had put weight on and no longer looked like he was 90 years old. He came by more often and offered to put a down payment on a house for her. She knew just which one she wanted. They drove by the house, called the real estate office several times, and were not able to reach anybody. Finally, they found another realtor's sign on a house, called it, viewed the house and asked the realtor to show them the house on First Street that Selia was in love with. She called it a "grampa grumps" house. It was from the outside very similar to the first house she ever bought. The minute she walked in, she knew it was the house she wanted. The first house was built by her father but did not know that fact until after it was purchased. She knew both were right because the minute she walked into both houses, they enveloped her completely. This house had the same giant floor to ceiling front window, the same type of Sonoma stone on the front and was a solid block home. Bing, bang, boom, the offer was made, which was rejected and the counter offer was accepted, James got $30,000 out of hiding for the down payment. James was concerned that Selia was too hasty to buy this home and felt they needed to look around more to find something selling for less. Selia would not listen at all.

CHAPTER 17

—✕—

Another Moving Day and Beyond

The financing on the purchase of the home was coming along good, so Selia gave notice at her apartment. Because Selia's freelance business had only been in existence for three months and she was not able to show a long term financial background, she was forced to accept a hard money loan for two years. She did not care because she wanted the house. After two years, she was legally able to refinance to a loan with a good interest rate.

Moving day came along and James's sponsor from AA helped with the move. James brought over some of his things. It had not been a year yet since James's hospitalization and only 9 months since she moved off the boat so Selia could not understand why James assumed he could move in.

Oh well, he did put up the down payment, was looking good again, staying sober and it was nice to be in his arms again. The lovebirds had been in their new home for only one day when the house phone rang. Selia answered with a very cheerful hello. It was the sister on the other end. The cheerfulness immediately went out of Selia's voice as she screamed why are you calling this phone number. The sister said she just wanted to talk to her brother. Selia viciously responded she was never to call the home phone again and if she wants to talk to her brother she was to call his cell phone and she hung up with a slam of the phone down on the cradle.

James had regained his swagger that Selia so loved. However, living with a newly sober person is as bad as a living with a person who just quit smoking and you still smoke. He constantly attempted to get Selia to quit drinking, which was always followed up with "it's not my problem." His final attempt was in the form of AA speak. He came home from an afternoon meeting and told Selia that he just found out he should not be living with someone who drinks, her immediate response actually shocked her because she did not take even a few seconds to think about it. Her response to James was "Oh, that's too bad. When are you leaving?" Selia wished that had come up a year earlier because after it did James finally settled in to living with a person who has a cocktail now and then and never brought up the subject again.

Selia's freelance business was booming. Each month she brought in no less than $8,000 a month and most of the time more. James became her househusband. It was not easy for him to swallow at first, but once he saw how much easier it made his bride's life, he actually began enjoying it. This brought them closer and closer together. Eventually she started taking him with her to certain projects. She introduced him to the main players in the City jurisdiction she was working on at the time. They all seemed to respond well to him so she finally informed them her husband would be making all the submittals and working on the projects in their jurisdiction.

The time came for James to work on his own on the development projects he had been following with his bride. She was going to send him to the City of St. Rose so she sat him down and gave him three items that needed to be taken care of. She went through each item with him on what needed to be done and how to do it. She felt great and knew he could accomplish it all. That evening when each arrived home Selia asked James how it went. He said it went great and went over Item #1, then went over Item #2, and then he said he didn't do Item #3 because he didn't feel it was the right way to handle the situation.

As they both were in the kitchen working on dinner preparations Selia's response was to ask him to sit down. She then proceeded to inform her husband/employee that when she assigned him the three duties it was as his employer speaking not his wife. She informed him he would be making another trip to St. Rose in the morning to take care of the third item he had been assigned to do and the way he was instructed to take care of it.

The next evening the kitchen scene starts again. This time James reports he had completed Item #3 the way she told him to do, and then he apologized to his bride who was 100% right AGAIN. James continued doing the work on the St. Rose projects, which gave Selia the time to work on two other projects in a different city.

Eventually, Selia had James assigned as the assistant site superintendent on a subdivision project in Racine. It was a little bit over an hour from their house. James had been diagnosed with macular degeneration and found when it was still dark in the morning as he left for work, he had to wait for a large semi-truck and then follow right behind in order to safely get down to the freeway. Once it was daylight, he did not have any problem. James finally told Selia about this situation and they decided to get him a motel so he did not have to drive in the dark. He stayed there Sunday through Thursday but they paid for the room for the entire week. This way he only had to bring home his dirty laundry and left all his other personal items in his room.

On Friday, James would head home well before dark. When he reached the Tower Bridge, he would call Selia and report that he was going over the Bridge. Selia would say "I'll meet you there," meaning their favorite restaurant in a small town in the delta called Roberto's Restaurant. It was a Mexican/Chinese/American restaurant. Roberto was of Mexican descent, his wife was of Chinese descent.

The couple met there every Friday for almost a year. The two used to go there when they lived on the boat so they were known to the owners and staff. They always ate in the bar because the restaurant was too big and noisy. They would walk in the bar entrance and by the time they got to their favorite table, Selia's margarita, James's coffee and hot tortilla chips and salsa were already at the table. Each week they debated about Chinese or Mexican. Sometimes they ordered both and shared. Depending upon the time of the year, they would order a side of deep fried asparagus. The asparagus was grown locally and every year they attended the Asparagus Festival in the delta area. At this point, their monthly income went up to between $15,000 and $18,000 a month.

This was such a fond memory for Selia and then suddenly she was swept back into the reality of her current life of emptying catheter bags and dispensing morphine. She did her good wife duties, fed James, kissed him, spent time cuddling him and went back down memory lane when he was settled down.

After remembering their every Friday meeting at Roberto's, she was reminded of when they still lived on the boat. One Sunday at 3:00 in the afternoon, Selia called out to James; said she was hungry and asked if he wanted to go to Roberto's. He agreed so off they went. They sat at the bar, Selia drinking margarita's and James drinking coffee (he was in his pretend to not be drinking stage). Lots of fun people came into the bar and everybody was playing the computerized Keno game. The couple actually won some money that day. The Mayor of the small town bought them drinks; they ordered dinner; ate as much as they could and left with doggie boxes in Selia's hands.

It was already dark when they left Roberto's. The marina where they lived was only about 10 minutes away. Selia was ahead of James as they walked down the dock to the boat because James was a slow walker and Selia was a fast walker. She reached the boat first, held the two boxes of left overs in her left hand, reached for the railing and attempted to step on the boat at the front door. Oops, she missed and her left leg went between the boat and the dock and as she fell, she was hanging onto the railing that forced the boat to hit her leg.

James rushed over to help her, laughed because she still had the doggie boxes in her left hand and helped her up and into the boat. She was wearing shorts and noticed blood running down her leg. James played medic and did the cleaning of the wound and the bandaging. The next morning she went off to work and the wound was not bothering her at all. James changed the bandage every night when she got home. The wound did not cause her any pain until Friday. It was "casual Friday" so she was wearing jeans. She started to notice every time she got up from her chair the wound would hurt because her jeans would rub against the bandage. Later in the day, the entire leg would hurt every time she moved.

Early Saturday morning, James helps Selia to the car and takes her to the emergency room to have her leg looked at. The doctor finally arrived, took one look and said there was a raging infection going on. He asked how it happened. When Selia told him how and where the wound happened, the doctor actually pulls back in revulsion, squeaking out eek. He said the delta water is the nastiest water around. He called in the nurse to give Selia a shot, clean the wound, bandage it and off he went never to be seen or heard from again. Her leg finally healed, but to this day, she has a deep scar on her leg.

After the infection incident, they no longer swam in the channel or put the fishing pole out at night before going to bed in hopes of catching a large catfish for dinner the next night.

— ✕ —

CHAPTER 18

Off Road Race Team

It was not all work and no play for the couple. James's best friend John, from AA owned an off-road race truck and race season just started. The first race for the season was called the Vegas to Reno run. Selia found out that the group of men who did the races did not allow "women" to attend. James wanted his bride to go along with him so he told the truck owner he would not help if he could not bring his bride. The owner agreed to allow the first woman to attend their race adventures. That's when Selia became an official member of the Chase Team. As it turned out, all the men were very happy about it. They found out that Selia filled a large ice chest with homemade finger foods, which they all loved. In the past, the men would stop at a 7-11 store to buy a loaf of white bread, bologna and mustard. That is what they ate during the race at the pit stops.

The group all set off together on Friday morning. Instead of going directly to Las Vegas, the group did the race direction backward from Reno to Las Vegas so they could spy out where the pit stops actually were. They stopped at each pit stop to check it out. One of the stops was the Bunny Ranch. Selia had to pee really badly and the men told her to come with them into the Bunny Ranch where they were going to get coffee. She refused to go in. Luckily, there was a ten-foot high pile of dirt she went behind.

They arrived in Las Vegas at the a favorite hotel and casino. They always chose this hotel to stay at because it was not near the Strip and it had a very large parking area where all the trucks pulling trailers with their off-road vehicles could easily park. On Saturday morning, the off-road vehicles were taken to another casino with a large parking area where the racecar inspections were done and a lot of hoopla went on. Selia loved the atmosphere and James was happier than ever that she was with him.

Sunday morning between 5:00 am and 6:00 am, the team met at the start line. With everyone present, Selia walked around with sandwich bags filled with squares of sausage frittata, mini cream puffs filled with tuna salad and other finger foods. The white bread and bologna men were thrilled. Cha Ching, Selia felt as if she was in like Flynn.

The race participants were sent off the start line in 10-minute intervals. Once the race truck was sent off, the Chase Team sets off on the regular roadway to the first pit stop. Each vehicle had CB radios. This way, team members could hear the racers status; whether the race vehicle planned to stop at each pit stop, and what they may need. Each member of the Chase Team had specific jobs assigned to him or her. James and Selia were assigned as the window washers and took care of feeding and cleaning up faceplates for driver and rider. This meant when the truck came in James went on one side to the driver; Selia went on the other side to the rider. A bite size candy bar was opened and put in their mouths, new water bottles or Gatorade was placed in their cup holders and a warm towel was used to wipe their face and then the helmet mask. There was not windshield to wash. The young men did the tire changing and the other heavy lifting duties. Selia offered more homemade treats at each stop to the chasers. How fun it all was.

This routine continued at each pit stop and yes the pit stop at the Bunny Ranch was hit and the men went in for fresh coffee again after the race driver was sent off with their needs taken care of. It was 12:30 in the morning when the race team crossed the finish line. We all stayed until all racers came in and the awards were handed out. Next stop was the hotel and a shower. Selia, no matter how dirty she was, collapsed on the bed and that was it until the morning.

This turned out to be such fun for the couple they started leaving on Thursdays by themselves and meet with the team on Friday evening when they arrived. The races were about once a month and Selia knew each time they did this their monthly income was down by a minimum of $2,000. This did not bother either of them as it was something they really enjoyed doing together. There was only one race Selia was not able to make. She found out later the white bread and bologna boys were not happy about it. Then they found out Selia did make goodies for them to eat even though she could not be there. The Baja 500 in Ensenada, Mexico was especially fun and other women finally started attending with their man. We all stuck together on this trip. The caravan crossed the border at Tijuana; followed the coastline road south to Ensenada. It was an extremely beautiful, scenic route. On the return trip, the caravan took a different route back. Rather than going through the border at Tijuana, our leader John, who owned the race truck, took us to a different border because he felt the Tijuana crossing would be very crowded. We were allowed across the border and then stopped after crossing by the Mexican Border Patrol. We saw a large motorhome being inspected by the Mexican Border Patrol. The owner of the vehicle was screaming at the Border Patrol and jumping up and down. When the Border Patrol approached our vehicles, John pulled out a carton of cigarettes, handed it to the headman and he waved our entire caravan through. Wow, just like you see in movies.

CHAPTER 19

—✕—

Life Style Change Coming Up

The couple continued as members of the chase team for the rest of the season and the next season's Vegas to Reno run. The time had arrived for James and Selia to discuss another change in life style. Their income from the consulting business and investment in natural gas wells skyrocketed that year. The project James was working on was finished so he had plenty of time on his hands. That is when James was diagnosed with beginning COPD and had a hard time breathing at times. They did notice when they were in the desert for the races he was able to breathe much better. They had been living in the area for almost ten years. It was a very humid spot which was part of James's breathing problem. Their home was two blocks from the Sacramento River and they could see the tall ships go by from their front porch. The other problem that affected his breathing was the smell of sewer sludge. The City gave the local farmers permission to use the sludge as fertilizer. The smell was extremely obtrusive.

James and Selia talked extensively about moving to the desert. James knew how much she loved their home. They had just remodeled the kitchen and it was beautiful. His bride had just re-decorated the master bedroom into an oasis of softness. This was especially important because the entire house was very hard with all interior walls being concrete blocks. It was an AWE moment every time someone entered the room.

James's health was getting worse and Selia made a big decision. She told James they could live very well on what they have been sending to the IRS and State in taxes. Selia was never a person motivated by money. It was nice for a while to have enough money to pay cash for the kitchen remodel at a final cost of approximately $40,000 and the softening of the master bedroom for a cost of $6,000. Money had never been her top priority. After much soul searching, she finally told her loving husband she would rather have her husband than the house she so loved and she meant it.

Since they had been at races in the desert areas often, they decided to look at the desert areas in Southern Nevada and North Western Arizona. Selia started doing computer searches, found a few she wanted to look at, hired a real estate agent in Arizona and the race was on. They made an appointment with the realtor, decided to get there a day before the appointment so they could do some looking by themselves. James chastised her not to fall in love with the first home she sees as she did with the home they now own. The glaring item that Californians take for granted was there were no gutters on homes in Arizona. Selia kept wondering why none of the homes in the area had rain gutters. Most of the newer homes in the area were stucco and the stains coming off the eaves on the stucco was not attractive. They drove by the house that Selia found on the internet and loved the outside of the house. The problem was the neighborhood was filled with old trailers. They decided to go to lunch and stop for the day. They found this off the main drag yellow house looking restaurant.

On the way in, Selia picked up the local real estate magazine. She found a listing for a home in Valley of Flowers. The waiter came to take their order and she asked him where Valley of Flowers was located. The waiter explained it was about 20 miles east on the other side of the mountain. Selia read the listing aloud to James. It read: 2,100 sq. ft. manufactured home on 5 acres; fenced and cross fenced; electric gate opener; 3 car garage; front portion fully landscaped with watering system; 4 bdrm/2 bath. Home comes with built-in big screen TV. Price $205,000. That was all James needed to hear. He loved it already.

The next morning they met with the realtor in Arizona. The first thing they did was show their realtor the listing in Valley of Flowers. She made a phone call to the listing agent and then off they went. Upon arrival, James said WOW. He fell in love with the property before even going in the house. Selia was not crazy about the house, the kitchen had very few cabinets; the guest bathroom was very small, but what she did like was the covered front porch and the 10X30 foot covered raised patio. The master bedroom was huge because it had a large sitting area as well as bedroom area and the other three bedrooms were on the other side of the house. There was a caretaker staying at the house who was a good friend of the listing agent. James asked him if they were to buy the property, would he stay on living there. James explained that he would be coming alone as his bride would be staying in California until their home sold so it would be good to have someone around who knew the area. The caretaker took James up on his offer.

They went back to the office in Arizona where an offer was written up. The realtor explained there had been another offer of $185,000 that had previously been accepted but fell through due to financing. James and Selia offered $185,500 with a sixty-day close. Bing, bang, boom the offer was accepted. That night back at their room at Harrah's in Laughlin they called their neighbor to let them know they bought a house. Selia asked where they were at that time because the call sounded sort of hollow. The neighbor laughed and said, "We are all partying at your house with Bill and Misa. Their house had a full basement. The garage was first so when you parked it was like parking underground; then a large open basement storage and workshop area. The stairwell came down from the laundry room and the other side of the stairwell was a living room, full kitchen, bathroom and one bedroom. The basement kitchen fridge was always filled with the neighbor's favorite beer and they all knew it. Apparently, the neighbors had been partying there ever since they had left. Selia laughed and told them they would be home the next day. Their neighborhood was very close and they did this type of thing all the time.

Each trip down memory lane brings other memories. She was reminded that she could not figure out why the living room area in the basement apartment of the home had so many wall electrical plugs and they were all half-way up the wall. The next-door neighborhood was a lovely lady who had lived next door since she was a child. Her home was newer because the original house burned down. She reported that our home had been used as a casino. The large storage workshop area in the basement was the place for the card tables. The living room area of the basement with all the electrical plugs was the slot machine area. The owner at that time would have people come from San Francisco on a boat. He would pick them up in a limo at the pier and take them to the casino. The house was built in 1948 and was still beautiful. The neighbor told Selia when she was about nine or ten years old is when the casino closed. She was out front one day and slot machines were being rolled out and up the driveway to the street. One of the workers asked her if she wanted one.

Even though it was a nine-hour ride back to their home, James and Selia loved their road trips and they always had to make at least one U-turn to make the trip memorable. When they finally arrived home, the neighbors came over and they all partied together in the basement. The neighbors wanted to hear about the new house.

——×——

CHAPTER 20

Bad News on the Health Front

During a routine health exam, James was diagnosed with fast spreading prostate cancer. Our health insurance was with a large HMO. The first thing required of prostate cancer patients was to attend a seminar on different types of prostate cancer, procedures and what to expect after surgery or radiation treatment. James and Selia found the room where the seminar was being held at the hospital in Walnut Creek. They went in and sat down. Selia noticed all the other men were being kissed by their wives, then they entered the room while their wives sat down in chairs provided in the hallway. She was the only woman in the room. She was shocked – why wouldn't the wives want to listen to the seminar. Selia could not imagine not wanting to learn about what her husband would be going through, after all, she would be the one helping him recuperate so they could continue their life together.

James was referred to a radiation treatment medical center that the HMO contracted with. After listening to the doctor for an hour, finding out radiation treatments would be 5 days a week for 6 months, James told the doctor thanks, but no thanks. He would rather have his prostate removed and be well within a few weeks rather than 6 months of treatment. James often talked about the actor Jerry Orbach who was on Law and Order. He continued to work in the TV series while having the radiation treatments and his deterioration was being shown on the screen then he died. Also part of James's decision was that they had just bought a new home and would be moving after the 60-day close of escrow.

They scheduled the operation for mid-March. The operation went well and Selia nursed him back to health. His after surgery appointment was 2 weeks after release. James told his Doctor he would be moving to Arizona as soon he was given the okay. The Doctor was extremely surprised how well James was doing. He exclaimed that James was in better shape after surgery as a 65 year old than the 30 year old in the waiting room. Selia chalks his fast recuperation up to the liquid vitamins they had been taking for the last year. As it got closer to and after the surgery, Selia double dosed James with the vitamins. After one more visit two weeks later with the Doctor, James was released to go ahead and move to Arizona. At this time, James confided to the Doctor he was still able to have an orgasm, which actually surprised him and he was not having most of the other side effects. The Doctor laughed and told James to just enjoy it as it is extremely rare but does happen if certain nerves are not cut.

Therefore, another moving day began. The neighbors loaded the spare bedroom double bed into James's truck bed, his clothes and personal items in the back seat and the dog's giant bed into the passenger side front seat. The next morning, James and Tony (the giant yellow lab that was James's 2nd love) got into the truck and off they went. Selia often laughed about her status in James's heart. She always said first came the truck, then came the dog and she was third on the list of his loves.

As they drove away, Selia laughed aloud about how the dog and truck actually came about. She also thought about how James was so extremely proud of himself that at the age of 65 he started a completely new career in his wife's business and did a great job. She watched her family driving away with her heart filled with love for her husband and could not wait to get to Arizona to join them.

One day, James left a message on Selia's cell phone. He said he would be at a meeting when she got home from work and warned her to be careful about opening the laundry room door because there was a big dog in the room named Tony. Okay, this should be interesting. Selia walked into the kitchen, pulled out a chair from the table, heard a big bark from the laundry room, opened the door slowly and part way, backed up and sat down on the chair. This large, shy, shabby looking dog slowly came out, walked up to Selia, and just looked at her with her big brown eyes. It was love at first sight – just like falling in love with James except he was not shabby looking.

Where did Tony come from? The neighbor across the street owned the bait shop at the pier downtown. Susie called James to tell him she just had a young man come in with a picture of his dog that he could not keep anymore. The picture showed Tony on the cement floor in a basement. The landlord did not allow renters to have dogs so the basement is where he kept his dog.

James, upon seeing the photo, arranged to pick her up immediately. Their love affair began immediately. Vet visits, professional wash, immediately rigged the truck bed of his Tundra with a dog leash attachment. James would take Tony every morning on a ride in the back of the truck to a levy. He would stop, let her jump out of the truck and then drive away about 5 miles an hour. Tony would run following the truck and when the trail ended at the water's edge, she would jump in and swim around. When she came out of the water, James lowered the tailgate, Tony jumped in and they drove home. This was an every morning event and both participants in the ritual loved doing it.

When the couple first moved into their new home, they had many plans on remodeling the kitchen. The kitchen cabinets were the 1948 metal models. One day Selia decided to take everything out of them and clean them thoroughly. With hot antiseptic water ready, she started cleaning the first one and nothing was happening. After a few scrubs she poo-pooed that idea and put everything back in the cupboards. When James returned that evening, she told him it was time to remodel the kitchen. He suggested they think about how they want to do it a while longer.

When James returned home the next evening, he was not surprised. Selia greeted him with a hammer, crow bar, and a broken tile in her hand. He laughed and said, "I guess we will be starting to remodel." He was always so willing to make sure his bride was happy in every way. He learned before they were married his bride was not the type of person to be told what to do. In his eyes, she was the strongest woman he had ever known. His type before Selia was the woman who needed a man to tell them what to do all the time, which meant he was in control of their entire life together. Not with Selia. James enjoyed her independence, ability to think on her own, and not be in need of a man but wanted to be with him. Every day there was a surprise of some kind living with his bride.

James and Selia did all the work except for the electrical upgrade in the kitchen and electrical installation of new appliances. They also hired James's AA sponsor, Kevin, to help with the heavy stuff or when needed. This was the beginning of the end of James's friendship with Kevin. Selia was getting ready to leave when she asked James not to leave Kevin alone in the kitchen doing work without supervision. James could not understand why. Selia told James, when he was not around, Kevin would do very sloppy work and would be very disrespectful toward her and he only did it when James was not around. Kevin was sealing the granite tiles on the top of a counter when Selia walked in and saw that he was dripping the sealant down the front of the white cabinet and asked him to be more careful. Selia was quite surprised with his response because he was only sarcastic to her when James was not around. Oops, Kevin made a big mistake. James stood up and exclaimed, "nobody talks to my bride like that – get out of our house now." Kevin left grumbling all the way to the front door. James was shaking. He was in shock that someone who had been such a strong and caring sponsor would do what he did. The next morning the Mercury was parked in front of the house. The couple had loaned it to Kevin so he would have something to drive and they did not ask for it back.

It took them an entire year to complete the project but it was not a big inconvenience. They did it section by section and completed each section before moving on. They started with the laundry room. Selia wanted to tie both rooms together so they did the country kitchen look in the laundry. It came out beautiful so the same look continued into the kitchen. When the house went on the market for sale, a realtor during the realtor showings commented to Selia how beautiful the kitchen was and he had not seen one as nice in a long time.

When the house finally sold, James told Selia "you were right, again." He felt they paid too much for the house, Selia insisted they did not. They bought the home for $192,000 and sold five years later during the real estate boom for $465,000 and then took off for Arizona.

Now the story how James's love affair with his Tundra started needs to be told. When Selia would do city clerk work for the City of St. Rose, she would work there three days and stay at her niece's house two nights in order to avoid the hour and a half commute every day. On her third day that week, she drove down St. Rose Avenue to get to City Hall and saw at a car dealership four new PT Cruisers. This was the time when the waiting list to get one of those cars was over a yearlong. She left work at 3 pm and stopped at the dealership. Told the salesperson she wanted the silver blue PT. He immediately told her they were selling for a premium. She said she didn't care, took a test drive, loved the seat and easy ability to get in and out and it had all the bells and whistles included. He took her into the office to explain the large premium of $10,000 over selling price. He finally got the message when she said, I don't care, write it up. She called her insurance agent to get it immediately insured. The salesperson ran the credit report, wrote the sale up and she was out of there in an hour and home at her usual time.

When James got home, she asked him if he parked his car in the garage or on the street. He was driving his mother's old New Yorker at that time and he parked on the street. Selia told him to go look in the garage. He came back, appeared to be a little ticked off and asked what was going on. She explained she bought it on the way home and left the '95 Mercury Grand Marquis at the dealership in St. Rose and he and his sponsor would have to pick it up tomorrow. James commented that the two of them should have talked about it before she bought a new car. Selia adamantly explained that they did because one day when they were driving down Hwy. 80 she saw a PT Cruiser and shouted, "I want one of those."

James pouted for a week like a spoiled child. He told the guys at the shop where work was done on the off-road truck what I had done and they said I could have had a Mercedes for that price. Selia said if she had wanted a Mercedes she would have bought one.

John, the owner of the race truck asked his son who was a car sales man (also the main driver of the race truck) in Ventura to look for a new Tundra for James. He found one with 2,700 miles on it that was a repo and told James if he wanted it he would drive it up north to their house and bring the sales papers with him. Of course, Selia laughed and told him to do it. The next weekend James was the proud owner of a 2000 Toyota Tundra with all the special items he wanted on it. Suddenly, he became a grown up man again as the spoiled child pouting stopped immediately.

That is the story of how Selia became #3 on the list of James's loves.

CHAPTER 21

The Final Preparation for the Arizona Move

Selia's husband and dog are down the road and now out of site. The movers had already been picked so Selia just has to call when she is ready to have their possessions moved to Arizona. The realtor has put a sign on the property and the listing is in the multiple listing. Upon reading the listing, Selia called her realtor and asked her to change the words "bonus room" in the basement and change to one bedroom apartment. The realtor was new and insisted that is how she needed to present it. After much back and forth Selia angrily explained either the realtor changed the wording or she would find a new realtor. After a few weeks and the wording had not been changed, Selia contacted the Broker about the matter. The wording was changed immediately.

Selia continued working on projects. She talked nightly with her husband, who she missed very much. All was going well in Arizona. As it turned out, the caretaker who was living at the house became an excellent roommate for James. Jay had triple by-pass surgery a few months back. The two of them became good friends and helped each other immensely.

Selia drove to Arizona once a month and stayed for a week. Each time she would fill up her truck with items she had packed. For the most part, what she packed was mostly unessential items not needed to keep the house looking good for potential buyer showings. At that point she had three of the cheap ceiling fans taken down from the Arizona house and switched with the expensive ceiling fans from the California house. The fan switch was actually done before a prospective buyer saw the expensive fans. Getting the fans installed in Arizona was not an easy feat. James was told by a few of the locals that things moved on Tijuana Time in Valley of Flowers. James made an appointment to have the electrician come to the house during the week of July 4th because his bride would be there and bringing with her the fans. After hearing about the Tijuana Time for the area, Selia insisted James call the man weekly to remind him when he was going to install the fans. As it turned out, on the day and time the electrician was to show up, he did not. James called and left messages and finally the man called back. He apologized and said he just walked in and just got back from his family vacation. He did make it over that day – James and Selia gave him no choice because they were not going to give in to Tijuana Time.

It was not until late August that the house in California finally sold. She called the moving company to set the date for pickup. The next time she went to Arizona, Selia walked through the house with a pad of post-it-notes and placed them on walls marked with what piece of furniture was to be placed in that spot. She did not want to leave the decorating decisions up to two men living like bachelors. A few things were a little off mark, but they were not the heavy pieces of furniture.

Once the movers took everything out of the house, Selia looked around and noticed some of the rooms needed to be repainted. At that point, she was sleeping on an air mattress. She only kept a small folding chair, TV tray table and a small TV they had used on the boat. Even though the house was already sold, she did not want to leave the house looking bad. So the painting began and Selia hated every minute of it as she was doing it.

When Selia went to Arizona the week of the 4th of July, she had a holiday bar-b-que so she could meet some of the new people James had met. It was a small crowd of only about 10 people but Selia loved entertaining no matter what. She was talking about how good her raspberry bushes were doing. James and Jay together fenced an area alongside the garage and planted them for her. They just had one small corner to finish the fence. Selia asked James not to do it until she got there the next week so she could be part of it. When she took the other ladies out to see her raspberry bushes she was shocked. The cottontail rabbits had eaten them down to nothing the night before.

Selia found herself wanting to step on the gas when she saw one of the cute bunnies in the road. Instead, she swerved so she did not hit one. The first morning after she officially arrived in Arizona she planted a box full of hens and chickens around the two shade trees in the front yard. The next morning they were totally gone thanks to the cutest little bunnies you could ever see. She actually found herself one night after midnight in her bathrobe sitting on the back porch with a high-powered flashlight. She sat down, lit a cigarette, turned on the flashlight and pointed it to the back fence. Staring at her along the back fence line was at least a 50 foot wide group of little beady eyes all ready to go through the chain link fence and feast. OMG, she laughed, understood finally what she was up against and went back to bed.

The neighbor across the street in California was also planning to move to Arizona when their house sold. When it sold, they asked if they could move in with James while they looked for a home. The wife and daughter went to Arizona while the husband stayed in California to work. He would go to Arizona whenever he could. James was all right with the situation because he loved that he could help them out.

—×—

CHAPTER 22

Finally Together Again in Arizona

Selia finally was able to move to Arizona. She arrived on September 30th. Even if the house did not sell by then she promised James she would be there no later than October 1st which would make it 6 months they were living apart. Selia put everything that was still in the house into the truck except for the air mattress she was sleeping on that night. In the morning, she left on the 9-hour trip from California to Valley of Flowers, Arizona about 4:00 a.m in the morning because she did not sleep a wink all night.

She had made the trip so many times. A particular gas station she always stopped at was at the base of the Tehachapi Mountains. She stopped, started pumping the gas and called James to let him know where she was and to tell him she was so sleepy she was afraid to drive much further. He told her to get a Red Bull drink, rest a little while after drinking it and she should be okay to drive.

Selia had never had a Red Bull before and noticed how small the can was so she bought two of them. She finished the pumping, pulled over to a parking space at the gas station, drank one of the Red Bull drinks, and just rested for about 30 minutes. It did not take long before she was feeling really refreshed, so she started on the road again. She drank the second Red Bull as she was driving. It wasn't long before she was feeling bright eyed and bushy tailed, wide awake and feeling good. She arrived at their home in Arizona at 1:00 in the afternoon and ran into the arms of her husband. He was as surprised as he was happy to have her with him again.

The first thing she noticed when she arrived was a garbage can in the kitchen overflowing with Pepsi boxes that were not broken down. Hell no was all Selia could think about! She did not say anything to the houseguests, but I think they figured it out when she immediately broke the boxes down and took the garbage out. The next day James and Selia went to an appliance store and purchased a trash compactor.

At that point, the houseguests had found a house to purchase that was on the same street but across the highway about five miles away. They had been trying to get financing since July but had such a bad credit rating they could not obtain financing. The other neighbors in California said they would help by purchasing the home and then rent it to them until their credit rating was good enough to get financing. That was taking forever because the neighbor was in the banking business and was looking for the best interest rate possible at that time.

Finally, James and Selia got the final escrow monies from the sale of their house amounting to $80,000. James told the wife that he and his bride would finance $50,000 for their purchase of the home, which was $100,000, and they could use the proceeds of $50,000 from the sale of their home for the rest. The houseguests said that was not enough because they did not want to use the money from the sale of their home. They actually had $60,000 from the sale in the bank. James said take it or leave it because that is all he will fund. The houseguests finally agreed to it.

Thanks to Selia's escrow knowledge the paper work was done, finances taken care of and the houseguests were out by the end of October.

Life in Arizona was good for the couple once the houseguests were gone. This did not include Jay. He was very welcome because he fit in like part of the family.

Before all the proper papers were signed Selia made sure the houseguests understood it was a business deal not a friendship deal and they needed to keep up with all the responsibilities of the note and deed of trust, keeping homeowners insurance with the James and Selia named as loss payee and the property taxes paid in full each year. If those things were not up to date at all times a notice of foreclosure would be sent to them. Well, guess what? Selia had to send them a notice of foreclosure three times. The friendship ended. They felt Selia was being unfair because they were having a hard time financially. Their payment was $450 a month. The wife worked full time for one of the local cities nearby and the husband worked in California making very good money.

James and his bride loved sitting on the front porch during the beautiful sunsets; during the monsoon's every summer and loved the ease of life they were finally enjoying. James loved to cook so he continued to do a lot of cooking. He decided he wanted to bake cookies so they bought a Kitchen Aid stand mixer. Because of his eye condition of macular degeneration, Selia printed out his favorite cookie recipes with large print. From a wise guy to a cookie monster, who could have figured?

It appeared his past was now in the past. Jay continued to live with them, which was fine with Selia. He had become an important friend to James and with the house being large with the master bedroom and sitting room on one side of the house and Jay's room on the other side nobody was in anybody's way. All three of them worked together to keep up the beauty of the existing landscaping. Selia was adamant on keeping James moving as long as she possibly could. Anytime he asked her to get him something from another room, she would refuse and tell him to get it himself. James knew what she was doing and did not mind it at all.

Jay often talked about going back on the road as a truck driver. He was getting restless. James offered to back him financially. We did that and Jay was on the road with a reputable trucking company where he leased a semi. Selia opened a special credit card so Jay would have money on the road. It was working out very good until Jay went to California where his granddaughter was having a baby and he wanted so badly to be there. After seeing his granddaughter and his new great grandchild, he left to go on the road again and his truck was found a few miles down the road from the hospital. He had a heart attack and died.

The owner of the truck sent his son out to get it. He was an extremely nice man and knew what we had done for Jay with financing his dream. He actually sent Jay's last paycheck to James in James's name. This resulted in paying off the credit card that Jay used. We had hoped to make money, but the important thing was we did not lose a dime, actually came out even. The best part was Jay died happy.

James's first visit to the emergency room was scary. He was having trouble breathing for a couple of days. The first time he had serious trouble breathing he was in the bedroom and called to Selia in a loud panic. She ran in and stated he was just having a panic attack. He immediately hollered out "panic attack, get a shot of brandy." The brandy worked. He immediately calmed down and was able to breath. This went on at least once a day for a couple of weeks. All of a sudden, he was in need of a shot of brandy many times a day. One night he was sitting at the kitchen table shaking and he could not catch his breathe.

Selia brought her car right up to the front door and helped James get in the car. Once they got to the emergency room, they took him in right away before other patients who had been there for a while because it was obvious he needed help immediately. When the first RN took his temperature, Selia asked what his temperature was. The nurse said he did not have much of a temperature it was only 100. Selia immediately corrected the RN by telling her his normal temperature was 97. The RN said thanks and got medication to lower his temp.

As it turned out, James had a bad case of pneumonia. He was in the hospital five days. Everyday Selia spent the time from breakfast through lunch with him or from the time of lunch through dinner. Of course, sleeping at night without him there was very difficult. When James was released, he was telling everybody that came to say good-by, the nurses, three doctors and discharge people he would never smoke another cigarette again. Listening to him tell all these people he would not ever smoke again, Selia knew was just another academy award winning performance. As Selia drove him home, she commented about his performance, and told him if he ever smoked another cigarette and he ended up in the hospital again, he would not come home when discharged; she would have him transferred to a nursing home.

All hell broke loose one day when Selia was looking for something on the back porch. Surprise, surprise, surprise, she found a pack of cigarettes and a Bic hidden in a drawer in the Mexican bar. James watched while his bride threw it all in the garbage.

The second time, a year later, James needed to go to the emergency room was an exact repeat of every event from emergency room visit #1, except one. The pneumonia was worse this time, so the lung doctor had him twice a day put on a machine that wraps a belt around his chest and shakes his chest using a speed appropriate for his age and frailty to break up the mucus.

One evening, a traveling nurse came into his room to administer the shaking treatment. She put the belt around his chest, turned the machine on and left the room. Well, that was not a smart thing to do. She did not check the chart for the appropriate speed to set the machine on, consequently it was on "bucking bronco" speed. The next morning James tried to tell everybody who came into his room that he had broken ribs. Finally, later in the day when the lung doctor came into his room James convinced him about the broken ribs by telling him he had broken ribs many times in the past and knows exactly how it feels. He was sent down to x-ray and, sure enough, James had three cracked ribs.

The hospital was extremely apologetic and did everything they could to keep the patient from filing a malpractice suit. One day, Selia was so exhausted she could hardly hold her head up while sitting in the chair next to James. He asked her to come and lay down in the bed with him. Before long, Selia and James both were sound asleep and for four hours at that. When they woke up, both felt so much better. The RN that was James's nurse came in and told them sleeping in the bed with a patient was not allowed. However, she said the both of them were so sound asleep she just pulled the drape around the bed and shut the door. It was the best sleep either one of them had all week. After a few more days in the hospital, James's doctors discharged him from the hospital to go home. Of course, Selia did not hold to her promise of sending him to a nursing home.

At this point, James's macular degeneration had advanced to such a point the only driving he would do was to the local small market down the road a few miles. When Selia returned home one afternoon James told her he would not be driving at all anymore. He explained when he started to pull out onto the highway to go to the Maverick he did not see a semi-truck coming at him but was able to stop in time and this frightened him to such point that he did not want to risk anyone else's life. His Toyota Tundra was then sold to the ex-houseguest's son for a price many thousands below blue book.

When Selia finally arrived to stay in Arizona, she and James would go "over the hill" (to the casinos in Nevada) every Monday morning before 8:00. His theory was to get there early before all the machines were reset after the weekend crowds are gone. Sounded stupid to Selia but it seemed to work. In the first six months, the couple had won $6,000 over what they had spent. Always at the same casino and the exact same slot machines.

Now that James could not drive anymore, Selia felt like it was even more important to make sure he gets out of the house so he would not get cabin fever. He was not using oxygen yet at that point so it was easier. On Monday's, Selia had to be at the model homes until noon. When finished she would go home, pull into the driveway, honk the horn and James would jump in her truck. At this point, James had been sober for nine years. The shots of brandy had not started yet. After a few times of picking James up, Selia finally asked him what he had been drinking. He exclaimed that he had just used mouthwash. A few days later, they were sitting on the front porch drinking coffee and reading the Sunday newspaper. Selia looked at James and asked him if he had anything he wanted to get off his chest. Even with more urging, his only comment was "not a thing."

With venom in her tone, Selia asked him "how f---ing stupid do you think I am?" He said he did not want to upset her and finally admitted to having a drink now and them. With a softened tone of voice, Selia consoled him by saying she does not care if he has a drink now and then, he will not be driving and must feel lost at times. She explained she was not as upset about his drinking when they lived on the boat as much as she hated the fact he lied about drinking.

After having that conversation, James openly fixed a drink for himself now and then. Selia was happily surprised because he never had more than one or two and she never saw him drunk again.

The couple continued their Monday trips to the casinos. James's lung disease was advancing fast. He was using the portable oxygen tank when needed, but it soon became a constant in his life. When Selia would take him to a casino, she would pull up in the valet area, jump out of the driver's seat and go to the passenger side to help James get out of the truck with his oxygen tank. They always played slot machines that were near the men's room so James would not have a long way to walk. These trips continued until after his fourth time in the hospital at which time Hospice became an important factor in both their lives.

CHAPTER 23

—×—

Another Life Style Change

Selia began watching their investment in natural gas wells as the investment started to dwindle. What used to be $6,000 a month income started going down every month. When the monthly income from the dying well was shrinking, Selia decided she needed to do something. She enrolled in a real estate licensing class that was on a fast track. Instead of having to go over the mountain to attend the class every day for 4 hours a day, 5 days a week, she enrolled in the 2 day a week class on Saturday and Sunday for 10 hours each day. She felt fine about leaving James all day as he was feeling good and was completely capable of doing for himself. Unlike California, Arizona did not allow taking the class on line which Selia had done 3 times, just never followed through with the licensing test.

The first day of class, Selia was thinking the instructor was quite a putz and he did not know what he was talking about. The second day the instructor started his instructional speech with "All the California people in the class need to forget everything you already think you know, you are in Arizona now not California." As it turned out the instructor was not a putz after all.

The class was a month long of 4 weekends. The last Sunday the final class exam was given. Out of 37 people in the class, only seven passed the final exam. Selia was one of them. She immediately went outside when she found out she passed and called the State Board phone number to schedule the next licensing exam. The testing date was scheduled for 2 days from then so she signed up. She did not want to forget a thing by waiting too long. The testing site was in Las Vegas.

The next day the couple drove to the outskirts of Las Vegas, got a motel room then proceeded to search out where the testing building was. Once found they looked for a casino near by the testing building where James could wait so he would have something to do. The next morning they checked out of the motel room, retraced their steps from the day before and Selia goes to the testing site. Bing, bang, boom, the testing took Selia 2 hours and she passed with flying colors. She called James to let him know she was on her way to pick him up.

James was bursting with pride for his bride. They celebrated by getting Selia her favorite drink, a margarita and calling Eldon to let him know she passed. Eldon was the selling realtor of the home they bought and the best friend of Jay who lived with them.

There were two choices for Selia at that point. Either wait for her license to come in the mail or go directly to the Real Estate Board in Phoenix to pick it up. Obviously, Selia and James made a trip to Phoenix the next morning. It was a three hour drive so they left very early in the morning; when they arrived there were no other people waiting to be helped so they were out of there and the horrible Phoenix traffic in no time.

She had been talking to the Office Supervisor of a large developer from Las Vegas about working at the models he had built in Valley of Flowers. She was told there would be a soft opening of the models next Saturday but it was not open to the public and she could not inquire about working at the models until the week after.

James knew exactly what his bride was going to do and he was right. The Saturday of the soft opening, Selia drove down to the models. As she was driving in, Mindy, the Office Manager, walked up to Selia's car and espoused, "I told you not to show up today." Selia immediately chimed in with "Mindy, I am an ex-project manager from California. I built subdivisions like this." Mindy did not hesitate at that point and told her to park her car and follow her. Selia was introduced to the broker and was hired on the spot. James's pride overflowed once again. His huge hug and kiss was all Selia needed every time.

She was suddenly reminded of the fact that she always believed men were born already handy and could wield any type of hand tool instinctively. James was the first man she had ever known that proved her theory wrong. The first time was when he had just moved into her duplex. He noticed the front porch light did not work. Selia knew it was only a loose switch connection and asked him to go ahead and fix it. After three days of futzing with it, Selia told him to stop, took the screwdriver out of his hand. She made sure the electrical connection to that switch was not on, proceeded to disconnect the switch, retightened the wire, put the switch plate back on and turned on the light. She had not taken care of it sooner because she lived there for many years; knew the approach to the front door very well and did not need the light. James did need the light turned on, as he was new to the home.

The next time James proved being a handy man is a learned trait, Selia asked him to replace the light bulb over the sink in the galley of the boat. The light cover was flush with the bottom of a cupboard. James looked and looked, tried to figure out how to get to the light bulbs, then gave up. Selia took over and replaced the bulbs. James was so frustrated he dove off the end of the boat into the channel between docks. He was an excellent swimmer. As he was swimming around, Selia asked him how he ever got small home repairs done. He said he didn't, he just hired someone.

Now she understood why he was so excitingly proud of himself after finishing the remodel of the laundry room and kitchen of the home they bought in California. She now also understood why it took an entire year and laughed about the lesson she learned. Not all men are born to be a handy man.

CHAPTER 24

—✕—

More Dying Hallucinations

The CNA was tending to James's needs. When she was finished bathing him she asked Selia if they had visitors the night before. When the CNA was informed there were no visitors she explained why she was asking about recent visitors. James related to the CNA that he had a great time last night. His brother-in-law Steven came to visit and stayed about two hours.

The next day when the RN arrived, Selia told her the story about Steven's visit and added that he had been dead for about two years. The RN, who Selia found was a very religious and spiritual person, explained to her that James's friends and people from his past were telling him it was okay to come and visit them and they were actually coming to bring him home.

This frightened Selia. She was not selfishly ready to lose her husband but also did not want to see him suffer anymore. Torn between two different feelings she again went down memory lane.

This time her mind went to James's drinking days while they were living on the boat. James had an evening meeting with a future employer in Sacramento. He had been drinking wine in the afternoon and appeared to be intoxicated when he needed to leave for his meeting. Selia begged him to call the man and ask for a breakfast meeting instead. James insisted he was fine and only had one glass of wine. Selia gave up and said fine, I hope you only kill yourself and nobody else. She truly did not expect to see him again.

Later that night a collect phone call came in. Selia accepted the charges and heard James's voice. He was in jail and wanted her to pick him up. Selia proceeded to use every bad name she could think of along with a whole bunch of profanity and then slammed the phone down into the cradle. She then picked up the phone and called her mother-in-law to tell her where her bouncing baby boy was. James arrived home about noon the next day. He walked in smelling like a cesspool. He explained he had been stopped by the Highway Patrol and lucked out by pulling into a fast-food parking lot and parked the car. He was arrested immediately for drunk driving and taken to jail. The next morning upon his release from jail, he had to walk seven miles to where the car was parked. This was the only good thing about the incident because the car was not towed or impounded.

Selia told him she called his mother and told her about his arrest. This was the only time she can recollect James ever being mad at her. She did not care how mad he was at her and told him so. She used a common saying – if you are going to play you have to pay for the consequences and she meant it. She chewed him out for quite a long time. The fact that his blood alcohol content was.21 and he kept saying that evening he had only one glass of wine was something Selia harped on for quite some time.

The legal process was very upsetting to Selia. Even though she was once a legal in the District Attorney's office and had been in the courtroom during arraignments of the same kind many times, this one really hit her hard. James was assigned a female Public Defender. When asked about his marital status he stated he and his wife were separated, he was looking for a job but was currently unemployed and had no means of income at the time. That was his sob story. They were not separated but he thought it best to not involve his wife. On his actual court date, he pleaded guilty. Selia had met the Public Defender and she immediately sent her out of the room so she could talk in private with James. It was obvious she had a crush on James. She only saw the smooth talking side of him.

After his plea of guilty, the Judge heard from the attorney relative to his indigent status and first time offender and sentenced James to 14 days of community service in lieu of a fine and attendance at a DUI class. Once the couple got outside the courtroom Selia broke down in sobs and was shaking. James tried to console her by stating how good the sentence was. She did not care and shouted, "This was the most humiliating event in her life watching her husband pleading guilty at the front of the courtroom and he should have listened to her when she begged him not to leave that evening." Talk about "a Teflon don." How does he do it? This incident was definitely marked on the calendar where Selia had been keeping his drinking episodes charted.

Even though the sentencing was light, it was still a financial drain on the couple. Their car insurance went up substantially, James lost his driver's license for six months, which meant Selia had to drive him to his nighttime DUI classes, which also cost over $300, however, he was allowed to drive to his community service program in in a nearby town which was about 30 minutes away. This was the turning point for Selia. She knew at that point if James did not make a total change in his life relative to drinking alcohol, she was definitely going to leave him. She reminded him she absolutely would not spend a lifetime of babysitting a drunk; that she has never done it and will never do it even for him.

This memory shocked Selia back to reality, back to current day in Arizona. This was not a memory she ever wanted to remember. She felt like she was only remembering the bad things about their life for the 17 years they were a couple. She remembered at that point, when they got married, she did not change her last name to his. She told him she was not going to do it until she knew he was "a keeper." Again, James just giggled and said that it was fine with him. It was coming up to almost two years of married life and James's birthday was coming up June 5th. The DUI incident had not occurred yet. If it had, things might have been handled differently.

CHAPTER 25

More of the Good Stuff

Selia was working in Suisun. She went to the Personnel Office and had her name changed in all records. She spent lunch hours going to the local Social Security Office to get a new card, going to the DMV for a new driver's license. Surprisingly, her boss let her order a new nameplate for her desk. It all came together so smoothly. For his birthday present, Selia handed James an envelope. James opened the envelope; looked at his bride with so much love in his eyes and gave her big hugs and kisses. That was when James found out he was a keeper. His present consisted of one piece of paper that was Xeroxed with a copy of Selia's paycheck, new social security card, her driver's license and her new desk nameplate all with her last name the same as her husbands.

When the couple bought their cute love nest it was named "Thumper" which was in large letters across the back of the boat. One afternoon James was on the back deck, Selia was in the lounge of the boat with the back window wide open. A woman at her boat across the waterway saw James and shouted out "Oh Mr. Thumper, Mr. Thumper." James looked up and answered her. She needed help with something so he walked over to her dock. They both hated the name Thumper, but could not come up with or decide on another name. Before James returned to their dock, Selia had jumped into the water with a razorblade in hand and removed Thumper off the end of the boat. A few months went by before a new name was decided on.

James's birthday was coming up again so Selia surprised James with tickets to see his favorite singer, Tina Turner, at the Concourse Pavilion. It was a great show. When Tina started singing her last song of the concert, James and Selia looked at each other at the same time and said "That's it." The next day they went to a sign lettering shop and had three signs made; one for each side and one for the back of the boat that said "Proud Mary - rollin' on the river." The signs looked beautiful and everybody who saw the signs loved it.

A few months later, Selia purchased her first laptop computer and got her first email account. Back in those days things were done much different than current times. She had to call the telephone company to get an email address. When they asked what would be the user name of the email, Selia immediately said Proud Mary. Then they asked for an 8 letter word for a password. She thought for a few seconds, looked down at the table and saw the eight letters on her Miller Highlife beer can. That was it, highlife was her password.

Selia felt better now and could end the memory lane trip for the day and spend time with the man who was the love of her life. She went into the bedroom and found James sitting up and very alert. He told his bride that he knew she always wanted to live in Tomales and he was willing to do it now. She felt he was very sweet saying that because on the day they bought the house in the small delta town, they were actually on their way to put in an offer on a house they had seen in Tomales. As they were driving down Hwy. 12, were only about 10 miles out, Selia told James to stop and turn around. When James asked why, Selia explained she knew his life was in where he had made many very good friends and she did not like how she felt when she thought about him having to start all over. Besides, she told him she had been driving by a house that she really liked in. They made a call to the Realtor in Tomales and notified him they would not be putting in an offer on the house on the bay.

Selia told him it would not be possible in his condition to make the move and he loved the people who always took good care of him. He agreed.

Because both James and Selia talked about his eventual passing, it was not an uncomfortable thing to talk about. Selia told James when he passed she was going to move back to California and settle in Tomales. He agreed and asked her not to make the move for two years. She never did find out why he wanted her to wait two years. She agreed, but shamefully, after he passed, she only waited three months before settling in Tomales.

—✕—

CHAPTER 26

More Memory Lane Bad News

The third time James needed to go to the emergency room, Selia was watching American Idol and looking forward to the last singer, her favorite. James walked out into the kitchen and sat down at the table. He asked for a shot of brandy because he was having a difficult time breathing after which he said he felt like he needed to go to the hospital. Selia retrieved the shot of brandy and told James they would leave when American Idol was over as there were only the last two singers left and she wanted to see the last one. Thinking about this when down memory lane it sounds like Selia was very insensitive to James's needs. She actually felt the exact opposite. Selia felt if she did not demonstrate an immediate need to rush out, James would start to relax, which he actually did.

Upon arrival at the hospital, the emergency room staff once again took him in immediately. All the usual RN's came in to take vitals and give him breathing treatments. By then James was feeling much better so when the next RN showed up and asked him how he was feeling he responded he was feeling much better but he could have died at home because his wife would not bring him to the hospital until American Idle was over. The RN immediately looked at Selia with her hands clasped in front of her chest and exclaimed "Adam Lambert?" They both giggled like school girls when Selia shook her head with a yes and a smile on her face. They both looked at James and he assured them with an okay

I knew I would not die and then he giggled. Again, he was always the happy person, never critical and always trying to please people, especially his bride.

Suddenly, Selia remembered the incident at the emergency room in California when James needed to have his gall bladder removed. The doctor that diagnosed his bad gall bladder had surgery scheduled for many months away. He did say though if the gall bladder became too painful and unbearable, to go to the emergency room and the gall bladder operation could be rescheduled at that time. About a month later, James was in such pain he could not walk from the bedroom to the kitchen.

Walla, let's not wait another three months, so off to the emergency room they go. Upon entering, the first line of communication at check-in, when asked, James responded "Hello, I fine today, how are you." With the next line of communication, same reaction. There were at least two more communication attempts by hospital staff with the same responses. James was being friendly and figured he would save his painful complaints for when he actually spoke with a doctor. NOT happening. What James did not realize, each one of the attempts at communication were for the doctors benefit and it was reported to the doctor the patient was in good humor and had no complaints of pain or feeling bad. Finally, a hospital staffer came into the room and reported the surgeon did not see any quality of life problems at this point enough to move the surgery up and the original date for surgery would remain on the schedule.

They had been at the hospital about six hours and Selia was frustrated. She told the staffer that she would like to see the surgeon. While waiting for the surgeon to come to James's room, Selia grabbed him by the gown and told him to stop being mister friendly and tell the doctor what is really happening; tell them you cannot walk from one room to the next because of the excruciating pain and everything else he was experiencing. Fortunately, the surgeon listened intently and decided there was definitely a quality of life issue to consider and he said he would do the surgery the next morning. James was then admitted to the hospital for the night and the gall bladder was removed in the morning. Lesson learned for both Selia and especially James – speak the truth from the first line of communication; do not worry about politeness at that point.

—✕—

CHAPTER 27

The Fourth and Final Time

Selia was in the kitchen when she heard James calling out to her in a very weak shout. She ran to him in their bed and he whispered he could not breathe. She handed him a shot of brandy which helped somewhat. He asked her to call 911 to get an ambulance to take him to the ER because he did not have the strength to stand up and walk to the car.

She did, the ambulence showed up; off they went to the hospital, she followed. The routine was starting all over again, only, this time Selia seemed to know it would be very different. Each time James was hospitalized, he came home feeling much better and could still walk around the house and do most things for himself. He was using the portable oxygen tanks at the time and was on it all the time except when he slept.

Just like the other three times, Selia spent as much time as possible with him at the hospital. She would be there before breakfast to help him eat and stay until lunchtime to help him again with his meal. Otherwise, the time spent with him would be lunchtime until after dinner. All this time spent at the hospital gave Selia a whole bunch of memory lane time. James would be awake only a small portion of the time while she was there, but each time he woke up he was very happy to see she was still there.

This time she is reminded of one of their dogs and how it came about that, he became part of the family. James's second love (Toyota 1st, Dog 2nd)

Tony, the yellow lab that James rescued was getting very complacent and not chasing rabbits off the property like she did in the past. James and Selia decided she needed a playmate to keep Tony active. Upon looking in the local newspaper ads for dogs, they found a lady giving away nine puppies. After calling, they went to the lady's house and saw all the puppies. Eight of the puppies looked as if they were brothers and sisters; one puppy looked completely different and was twice the size of the others. James told Selia it was her choice this time since he is the one who chose Tony. Selia went one at a time picking up each one. All the puppies were running around, trying not to get picked up, but one. One puppy sat at her feet the entire time waiting for his turn to get picked up. Finally, Selia picked up the puppy with all the patience. He was totally different from the other puppies. He was the one, obviously, that hit the food bowl before the other puppies could. Unlike the others, he was heavy and muscular. What Selia liked about him the most was he had a very calm personality. She looked at James, pointed to the calm puppy and shook her head YES. James was thrilled; that was the puppy he wanted the minute he saw him.

It took them a few days to come up with a name for the calm puppy. He was the cutest puppy Selia had ever seen and loved him from the beginning. His cuteness stemmed from the fact that no matter where Selia walked in the yard he was directly behind her. He followed her no matter what. One afternoon, the happy couple was sitting on the back porch. Selia jumped up and said she had to get something out of the garage and would be right back. As she was walking toward the garage, she hollered to James and asked if her shadow was behind her. She heard a loud "Yup" from James. That was it! The puppy finally had a name he could live up to – Shadow!

As it turned out, Tony did not like having a new friend in the family. She would growl at Shadow every time he got near James. When they would feed the dogs, Tony would run over to Shadow's bowl and growl at him if he tried to eat. Consequently, Shadow started lying down in front of his bowl and pretended like he was not going to eat. He would turn his head to look at Tony and if she was not paying attention, Shadow would take a bite. It would take a long time for Shadow to eat, so they had to stay out on the porch with the dogs until Shadow was finished.

Shadow was signed up on the puppy plan at a veterinarian office. This meant he visited the vet's office once a week. He loved his rides in the truck. While they would be in the waiting room, everybody who came in always awed over and over again about Shadow. He was incredibly beautiful, well-mannered and nobody, even the Vet could believe he was only three months old. He had the head, coat and jowls of a Newfoundland and the paws of a Labrador. The Vet did not want to neuter him for about a month, but said if he got up to 50 pounds the cost would be more. The day came; Shadow was weighed and yeah he only weighed 48 pounds. That was a lot for only being four months old.

Tony and Shadow each had their own large dog pillow to sleep on. They were next to each other under the workbench in the garage. They did sleep together in their own space. Shadow did learn from Tony and they eventually became friends, but Shadow never stopped eating his food lying down on his belly.

Selia came out of her memory lane trip when James woke up in time to have his breakfast. She helped him with his tray as she always has. She could see that he was not doing very well. He asked her if she would bring the next day some brandy, which he said works better than the morphine they were giving him.

After five days in the hospital, one of his doctor's came in when Selia was present and told James he could go home the next day. The doctor explained James was not getting any worse and not getting better either and they would rather see him go home than to pick up some other illness by staying in the hospital.

When the doctor left the room, Selia told James she had $200 in cash in her wallet and was going to go "over the hill" and not stay for his lunch to arrive. She had an overwhelming fear that their life was about to take a major change. As usual, James giggled a little and said for her to go have some fun for a change and he would see her in the morning.

Well, Selia did go "over the hill." She did not have her usual fun. She became manic; got more cash from the ATM three times using two different accounts, and just did not want to go home for a long time. She finally went home about 10:00 that night. In the morning, she filled a flask with some brandy and put it in her purse. When she arrived at the hospital James's breakfast was delivered; she helped him; he had a shot of brandy and waited to be discharged. Just getting into the wheel chair, being wheeled out to the truck and getting into the truck was almost more than James could deal with. He was not able to breathe very well so he took a sip of brandy. This always shocked him back into being able to breathe.

After arriving back home, Selia helped James into the house and to the bedroom. He was exhausted from the trip home. That was when James starting having a very hard time getting out of bed and to the kitchen. He started using a walker. It was only a week, maybe two, when Selia called the doctor and had Hospice prescribed. Bing, bang, boom, that was the start of what was yet to come.

Now that James settled into the bed and was resting nicely, Selia continued her memory lane trip vigorously in her heart.

———×———

CHAPTER 28

The End is Near

While at James's last doctor's appointment, after his fourth hospitalization in four years, Selia asked the doctor for an honest opinion on his condition and his probable life expectancy for someone in his current condition. At this point, James was not able to converse so he was very welcoming of Selia's inquiry. The doctor was very matter-of-fact in his response. He very clearly explained that in his experience with patients (he was the lung doctor) James's life expectancy most likely would be no more than six months.

When James was comfortable after returning from seeing his lung doctor, Selia took out two photo albums. There were many photos that depicted the fun parts of their life together in both the duplex in and while living on the boat for the most part. James was the person in charge of the handwritten comments about each photo. She could not stop laughing. She now wished she had pulled the photo albums out long before now because she felt like most of her memory lane trips seemed to be about the bad times rather than the good.

She had not even remembered the three ducklings that were orphaned because an extremely large seal that came up to the delta from the bay area was eating everything in sight. One day, Selia was sitting on the back deck and suddenly a huge seal jumped up out of the water. She and James were actually at the spot where the seal gulped up the mother of the three ducklings. They scooped up the ducklings and took them to their boat. They managed to keep them so well fed that the three little ducklings never went far from the boat. Selia named them Mini, Molly and Sarah. As they were growing, suddenly Mini's tail feathers started to curl – oops she was suddenly renamed "him" Mickey.

All the other boaters near their dock got a big kick out of watching Selia relate to the ducklings. The ducks were pretty much domesticated by that time. If Selia saw them way down at the end of the channel, she would call out to them with "come girls, come girls" and they would immediately come flying to the boat and swim around looking for food. This lasted for an entire growing season for the ducklings. Once all grown up they flew off to become adult ducks and James and Selia never saw them again. How fun, it was such a smile creating memory.

There were so many photos of the great times while living on the boat. The fourth of July, they would go with another couple on their boat to the wide-open waterway and anchor down where Howard Johnson's Motel would put on a huge fireworks display. There definitely were tons and tons of wild partying and grilling going on.

One afternoon, James asked Selia to sit down next to him. As he was holding her hand with a gentle caress, he proceeded to look at her with his loving eyes and told her he had been thinking a lot about when he dies and wanted her to know the only thing in his entire life he will miss is her, his bride. All of sudden he giggled like a little school boy; said "Oops – I'll be dead so it guess I can't." Selia knew what he meant and cuddled him for quite a while. She always loved his little giggle but his last giggle seemed very different.

She suddenly remembered his lung doctor tried to get James to do the sleep test because the doctor said he had sleep apnea. The doctor set up appointments three different times for James to go to a place and go to sleep. Selia would not allow it. She told the doctor repeatedly he did not have sleep apnea. She slept next to him every night; he did not even snore; he just had a slight whisper type of breathing and she was not going to allow him to go through that agony. The last appointment was when James had just learned he had a maximum of six months to live. Selia called the center where the test was scheduled; explained the circumstances and the director of the center agreed with her the test was unnecessary and did not need to be done. This was when she finally realized the doctors customarily ordered unnecessary tests if the patient had good insurance.

The daily routine with the RN, CNA and oxygen deliveries went on for five months. At that time, James started inquiring of the RN what it would be like when he died. He wanted to know if he would suffer when he was dying or would he just go to sleep. He did actually ask the same of the RN several times. Her answer was always the same. She very kindly and lovingly told him in her experience she always saw patients in his condition just quietly go to sleep without suffering. Whether or not it was true, James seemed very calmed by what the RN related to him.

Even though James was bedridden for all of the five months, using a catheter, he still forced himself to get out of bed to use the porta-potty that was directly next to his hospital bed for bowl movements. As time went on, he did occasionally ask for help getting in and out of bed.

Selia's volunteer helper from Hospice got in the habit of coming many times during the week. She was not necessarily there to relief Selia so she could go to town to shop for groceries without worry. The two of them had gotten in the habit of just getting together to play cribbage. James enjoyed hearing them hooting and hollering and often called out "who won that hand." Selia taught James how to play cribbage when he first moved in with her at the duplex. After their Sunday morning Bloody Mary's on the front porch, they would go to the kitchen table and start playing cribbage. James was a quick learner. Selia always knew he had a razor sharp mind. His mind was only one of the many things she loved about him. One of those Sunday cribbage games started around 10:00 a.m. and ended at 7:00 p.m. and they were still in their pajamas. They both saw absolutely no reason to bother getting dressed at that time.

It was one of the cribbage playing days. Selia and the volunteer heard James calling from the bedroom. They ran into the room and saw James on his knees holding onto the bed to keep him upright. They tried to get him off his knees and up high enough to roll him into bed and could not do it. James was not alert enough or strong enough to help us help him. The volunteer ran into the master bathroom and came back with a very large bath towel. They used the towel as a fulcrum and pulled on the towel that they placed around his belly. This gave the two ladies with something to pull him up by. As they pulled, they shortened the grip on the towel and he became higher up on the bed. Finally, he was up high enough to roll him into the bed. The only problem was that his upper body landed only to the middle of the bed and his feet hung over the end of the bed. No attempt to pull his body up to the top of the bed worked. Selia grabbed a pillow, put it over the foot of the bed and placed his legs and feet in line with his upper body.

They covered him with a blanket; made sure he seemed comfortable and made sure he was breathing. Selia was aware his regular RN would not be in, but the traveling RN from Texas would be coming in to see James. She was a much larger woman and seemed very strong. When she arrived, she did pull James up to the appropriate position in the bed without any problem at all. She commented that it is extremely rare for someone with his breathing problem to be sleeping on his stomach. Selia assured the visiting nurse that sleeping on his stomach was his every day way of sleeping and he is most comfortable when sleeping that way.

Selia would lift his chin and try to get some water into his mouth. She did this for two days and then the RN told her not to do it as he could actually choke. She explained his body was in end stage but was still resting very comfortably. He seemed to be breathing better than he had for many months. His soft whisper snore that was always so comforting was all she could hear. When she would pat his face and hear that soft whisper, she knew he was still alive.

A few days later, Selia received a phone call from her previous client, Tim. He asked her to meet him and Robert for breakfast the next morning at Harrah's Casino. She agreed to meet them and then called her Hospice volunteer who agreed to sit with James.

—✕—

CHAPTER 29

The End Arrived

She had breakfast with Tim and his friend, Robert, on Saturday. She remembers when he called to ask her if she would like to meet them at Harrah's. She immediately said yes – then regretted it.

The last time she saw them was about two years previously and she was two sizes smaller in jeans. Now, after the last year of doing nothing but taking care of her husband and eating ice cream, potato chips and dip every day, she had ballooned up to a whopping 194 pounds.

It was a fun visit while the three of them ate a leisurely breakfast. Tim made Selia feel good. He was always complimentary toward her. This time he said she was always like a ray of sunshine. He laughed when she told him that one of her nicknames from her father was Sunshine.

Just as they were finishing breakfast, Selia let them know her husband had been mostly comatose for the last four days and did not expect him to live much longer. The two men expressed their deepest sympathy and concern for Selia. She let them know she would keep them informed, thanked them for breakfast and said good-bye so she could go home and be with her husband. She did not want to be away from home for long because her Hospice volunteer was leaving early in the morning to go to the East coast to visit with her family.

It was a quiet afternoon and evening. Selia checked in every hour on James and he just seemed to be so completely at ease; breathing softly and easily. It was the fifth day of him not moving a muscle. He was still in the exact position as when the visiting RN moved him to the top of the bed. At 8:00 p.m., Selia started to walk in the bedroom to check on James and she could hear his easy breathing so she just walked out to the back porch for a cigarette. At 9:00 p.m., she was going to go out and finish the half of cigarette she did not finish the time before. As she approached the bedroom door, she did not hear James's easy breathing. She approached James, felt his face and immediately knew what had happened.

She left the room and closed the door, then immediately called her Hospice volunteer and told her she thinks James had passed and she was calling the RN on duty as soon as they hung up. The volunteer said she would be out to her house in a few minutes and no amount of objection from Selia would stop her. Selia did not want her to come out because she was leaving on her vacation at 6:00 in the morning.

Selia made the call to the RN on duty, she arrived within ten minutes and she verified James has passed. At this point, the Hospice RN goes into action asking questions of Selia. The first question was to ask if she wanted James's body to remain until the morning or have the mortuary pick him up that night. Her response was to have the mortuary come to pick him up that night. The RN immediately phoned the mortuary. She reported to Selia they were not able to do the pick up until very late that night. She was okay with that.

At that point, the Hospice policy is to cleanse the body of the deceased. The RN and the volunteer proceeded to wash James. Selia closed the door. She was adamant that she did not want to see her beloved husband not alive. When that phase of the Hospice policies were completed, the RN wanted to know if Selia wanted her to stay until the mortuary arrived. She did not feel it was necessary and did not ask the RN to stay.

The mortuary finally showed up at 1:00 a.m. Selia showed them to the closed door of the bedroom where James was. She explained she did not want to see them wheel her husband out in a body bag and she would be out on the back porch when they were finished. She and the volunteer went out to the porch and smoked a cigarette. Selia tried to tell the volunteer she did not need to stay but the volunteer insisted she wanted to, even though she would not get any sleep before leaving on her vacation.

Once everybody was gone, Selia grabbed a blanket and pillow from the guest bedroom and collapsed in exhaustion on the couch. She could not bring herself to open the door to the master bedroom, not yet anyway.

Obviously, Hospice does not leave anything to chance. First thing in the morning, at 8:00 a.m. Downtown Drug Store was at the house picking up all the equipment that James was using. The miracle of a Hospice prescription is Medicare pays for everything and the family is relieved of the worry of how to pay for the help. Once the equipment pick-up was complete, Selia went to the phone to call James's daughter who lived in New York. There was no answer so she left a message for Sarah to call. Selia did not feel leaving a message of death would be appropriate.

Sarah had been given the opportunity to come to Arizona to see her father before he died. Her Aunt said she would pay for the trip. For some reason, Sarah could not bring herself to visit her father. Her father was excited about the possibility of seeing his daughter. After her making excuse after excuse, he finally quit calling his daughter and his sister. Actually, he just did not use his cell phone anymore.

About an hour later, Sarah called. She said she did not hear the voice mail. Her reason for calling Selia was to tell her that her Aunt called the Sheriff's Department to do a well check on her brother because he was not answering his phone. Selia was a bit perturbed and exclaimed that it was too late for that; James had died the night before. Sarah's response was even more disturbing to Selia. All she wanted to know was when the funeral was because she would definitely be coming to the funeral.

The emotional distress Selia was feeling by then was roiling over the top. She reminded Sarah she had been told many times, there would be no funeral at her father's request. She wanted to chastise Sarah about not making a trip to Arizona to see her father alive, but will definitely show up to see him dead. She was not the type of person who would purposely hurt someone's feelings. Selia said good-bye to Sarah and walked toward the front gate. There was a Sheriff's Deputy getting out of his vehicle. Selia did not give the Deputy a chance to say anything. She expounded she just found out he was coming to do a well check on her husband; told him it was too late, he passed last night. She continued with her rage saying the woman who called was his sister who is a crazy dimwit and her husband had chosen not to talk with her. She calmed down and explained the Deputy was welcome to come in or he could call hospice and verify he had excellent care. The Deputy was quite considerate. He expressed he was sorry for Selia's loss and did not need to do anything further.

That night, after she had put the master bedroom back together completely as it was before all the hospital equipment, Selia slept in the room. It was late when she finally went to bed and she was very tired from all that had gone on that day. Just as she got into the bed and her head hit the pillow she sat up abruptly and looked around. She heard James's voice calling out Honey, just as he always called her for 17 years. As startling as it was, it was also very comforting. She had never believed in it before, but she now knew James was telling her he would always be with her.

As promised, Selia called Tim to let him know her husband had passed the night before. This was the beginning of their deep friendship. For at least a month, maybe two, Tim called Selia daily to make sure she was all right. This meant so much to her; there was nobody else who soothed her feelings from the loss of her husband aside from her two adult children. They were both very sad for their mother. Her son was very sad for his mother; he knew how much his mother loved James. Her daughter touched Selia's heart by sobbing how sorry she was; how she was going to miss him and how much he showed the world he loved her mother who was his whole life. That is what Selia always felt but finally admitted to the realization of the depth of the love between her and her husband.

James's daughter called again a few days later and asked about her father's will. Once again, the daughter only wanted to know what she would get. She was not happy with Selia's response of he did not have a will; what he did have was built up during their marriage and belonged only to her now; then she hung up the phone.

The Hospice volunteer came by when she returned from her vacation to see how Selia was doing. She asked when Selia planned to return to California. She responded she was not leaving until she sold her home and knew she had a very good home for her three large dogs. The volunteer immediately said she would buy the house and keep the three dogs. The two pups, Max and Muffin had already bonded with the volunteer. Selia was too busy taking care of James to worry about bonding with the pups as she had done with Shadow. They set a price for the property and laid out the details that the volunteer would refinance the home, but in the meantime, she would keep up the mortgage payments. A $10,000 down payment was accepted, and then Bing Bang Boom, Selia was free to prepare for her move back to California.

The two ladies had bonded for the last six months, so Selia suggested to the volunteer that she might want to go ahead and move into the house now. She did move to Valley of Flowers from her home on May 1st.

CHAPTER 30

The New Beginning

While working on all the final paperwork due to a death of a spouse, Selia started working on her eventual move. She started packing up the few things she would be taking with her and putting them in the garage. Any furniture she would be taking was also put in the garage. She made sure, that as she removed furniture, she rearranged the items left so the room would look like nothing had been removed.

Her search for a place to rent she did completely on-line using the local newspaper ads. She was getting discouraged; everything for rent in Tomales was much more than she could afford. She set $1,000 a month for rent as her highest limit. A friend suggested she try Craig's List.

The first try on Craig's List surprised Selia to the height of ecstatic happiness. There was an ad for a 2bedroom/2bath, upstairs apartment right on the bay. It was in the remodeling stage and would be ready by July 1st. The rent was $1,200 a month, but after the long search, she was willing to up her ante for rent payments. She immediately picked up the phone and made an inquiry. The person she talked to told her the ad had only been on Craig's List for 10 minutes. Negotiations began and ended with Selia getting the apartment for $1,100 a month in exchange for a two-year lease. The only thing she did not like was the landlord did not allow dogs. She was hoping to be able to keep Shadow with her. The move-in date was set for July 1, 2010. She made sure she let her newfound friend, Tim, know about her good luck. He was always very complimentary to Selia and told her he knew she could do it.

Knowing when the apartment would be ready to live in made picking the date to move back to California easy. June 29th, Selia rented a u-haul trailer. Friends picked it up with their large motorhome; drove over to her house; loaded it up with everything Selia had been storing in the garage. Her Toyota Tacoma was also loaded to the gills. The bed of the truck was loaded up to the top of the cab. The front seat and back seat of her truck was also filled to capacity. The next day, Selia led the caravan out the driveway and headed to California.

It was a thirteen-hour drive. They stopped for breakfast, lunch, dinner, and gas. Each stop was carried out for the minimum amount of time as possible. After thirteen-hours of driving, Selia pulled into Doran Park, the first campground near Tomales. The troupe spent the night at a campsite in the motor home. She was so exhausted; she did not actually fall asleep. She was lying on the couch trying to close her eyes but could not keep them closed. In the morning she was telling her friends about it and how her head and eyes were so screwed up she actually could see the wind blowing. She did not mean she could see the trees or plants blow in the wind. No, she could actually see the wind moving across the windows.

Breakfast, especially coffee, was first on the morning agenda. The moving troupe arrived at the marina where the apartment was at 8:00 a.m. The actual area around the marina was a bit on the tacky side, but the apartment was beautiful. Everything inside was brand new, which also meant it was squeaky clean. The entire front of the living room had wall-to-wall windows with a beautiful view across the entire bay. The two bedrooms were small but useable. The master bath was also small and the second bathroom was a very good size. Selia felt she would be very happy in her new apartment building because there were only five apartments.

Selia's kids and grandkids showed up to help move her belongings from the overloaded trailer and truck. The only items put where they belonged were the bed and dresser in the master bedroom. Everything else was just put in the living room to be taken care of when everyone was gone. By the end of the week, she had the apartment looking like a little dollhouse.

She settled into her new life very comfortably and loved everything about living in Tomales, as it had been a dream of hers since she was ten years old and her father would bring her to the bay to dig for horse neck clams. She was now 65 years old. A long time to hold on to a dream.

As time went by, Selia was enjoying her new life. She walked around the bay everyday between three and four miles. It was not long before the daily walking did the trick for losing about two thirds of the excess poundage she had gained while James was dying.

The only problem she had was James's daughter kept calling her and asking about some oil drilling rights that belonged to her father and her aunt. Selia explained she knew nothing about it and to check with her aunt. That was the time Selia decided to change her cell phone number to a local area phone number. Consequently, she never heard from James's daughter again.

——×——

CHAPTER 31

Her Heart Feels Broken and Finally Sheds Tears

Selia loved her new life. She was happy to be near her children and grandchildren again. She was also extremely happy to finally be able to see the San Francisco Giants baseball games on television. When living in Arizona, she could only see them when they played the Arizona Diamondbacks. When her kids were little, back in the mid 1980's, she took them to as many home games she possibly could. Tickets were easy to just buy when arriving at the ballpark because the Giants were the worst team in the National League. October 2010 changed all that. The Giants won the World Series. They had a giant parade in downtown San Francisco and Selia watched the entire event for five or six hours.

All of a sudden, she heard a loud gasp come from her mouth. The top executives of the Giants Corporation were being introduced. They introduced Brian Sabian who then went to the microphone to speak about the team and the great year they had. Shock overwhelmed Selia. The man just introduced had the same silver hair combed in a similar fashion as James, the same large head, wore the exact same glasses as James did and walked with the same suave swagger as James. She felt like she was looking at James. They looked so much alike. Finally, the tears fell and she began to wish he were with her, even if he was bedridden. Even their manner of speech was similar. The parade was replayed the next day and she watched every minute of it all over again, and cried again.

Her friend, Tim, stayed in touch with Selia over the months by email. The emails started to take on a suggestive attitude. It was probably Selia's fault because she missed having "Her" man in her life. Tim let Selia know he and Robert would be flying into Reno in January and asked if she would like to meet them there. He said he looked on a map and found Tomales was between three and four hours away and he would pay for her room. She agreed to meet them in Reno.

Selia drove up to the City of Brookshire to see a lady friend and spend the night with her. The next day, she drove to Reno, which was only two hours from Brookshire. She checked into her room, which was next door to the room the guys were staying in. She gambled for a while because the plane Tim and Robert were coming in on was not due for a few more hours. When the time for their arrival became closer, Selia took the hotel shuttle to the airport and got back to the hotel in a limo. They did not expect to see her until they arrived at the hotel. It was fun for all of them with the surprise at the airport. Tim was very warm and welcoming which started up that same old throb as the first time she met him.

Once the guys got settled into their room, the three of them went to the casino. Before going downstairs, Selia asked Tim why he had gone to Minneapolis in December. He explained he was visiting family and that he was born there. Selia asked him in what hospital he was born. No kidding was all Selia could say. She finally told him she was born at the same hospital ten years earlier and that was how she got her name by being born at St. Selias Hospital in Minneapolis. All three laughed at the coincidence.

The next day, the two men went off to do their gambling in other casinos. Selia stayed at Harrah's and gambled. She decided she was not going to stay the second night so the two fellas could do their own things. She already had such a heartwarming time with Tim and just wanted to bask in its warmth. She called Tim's cell phone and left the message that she was heading back to Tomales.

She stopped in Brookshire, spent the night at her friend's house and drank many margaritas. The two-hour drive home found her still reeling from the warm glow of romance.

The story does not end here.

—×—

CHAPTER 32

Writer's Finishing Thoughts

I did it! As I was writing the last year of my life spent with my husband, I began to feel like all I was writing about was the bad news days. In hindsight, now that I am finished going down memory lane, this writing was a wonderful experience that I desperately needed to go through.

My incentive to write this story was to bring his life back and tell all about him. Well, guess what? The further I got into telling "His" story; I soon realized it was more a story about Me.

Since his passing, I had only reminisced on all the good times we had together as husband and wife. I did not even think about the bad times we went through. The good thoughts always outweighed any of the bad. Consequently, I had built my image of him up to "God" status.

I feel very free after this experience. I no longer feel bad because I miss him so much. Instead, I feel lucky to have had seventeen years with him. I still believe he and I had a relationship that very few people will actually achieve, but now I can laugh about the real man I loved, the flawed human that was a genuine angel to me even though he misplaced his halo a few times. He fulfilled my dreams about love in every way possible by freely providing what I had never received in other relationships: Respect, Freedom to be Me and the loving look in his eyes whenever he gazed upon me. Sappy, I know!

I learned so much about myself doing this exercise. I only realized how long I have been a stubborn human being when I looked at my 1ˢᵗ grade school photo the day I completed my story. The school would not let me have my photo taken with my teddy bear and I refused to have my picture taken without my teddy bear named Bubby Bear. I won.

Thanks for reading my story. I hope to read your story someday.